HODDER 20TH CENTURY HISTORY

THE GREAT WAR

FOUNDATION EDITION

CONTENTS

→ **Key Issues**

- Why did war break out in 1914?
- Why did men go to fight in it?

Key Words

- alliances • hatred • Alsace–Lorraine • fear
- Franz Ferdinand • volunteered • patriotism
- Pals battalions • uniform • white feathers

In 1914, Europe was split into two sides:

- Britain, France and Russia.

- Germany and Austria–Hungary.

Look at the map and see where these countries were. We call these groups **alliances** because each group of countries had allied themselves together (made agreements to support each other if there was a war).

War broke out in 1914 because the two sides had hated each other for some time.

France hated Germany because in 1870 Germany had conquered a part of France called Alsace–Lorraine. Britain feared Germany's growing navy. Russia and Austria–Hungary were falling out about south-east Europe. *Everybody* feared Germany's growing army.

THE ALLIANCE SYSTEM

The long-standing hatred of the two **alliances** was the long-term cause of the First World War. But, of course, they had hated each other for years without war breaking out.

In June 1914, however, Franz Ferdinand, the son of the Austrian Emperor, was shot by a terrorist. This was the short-term cause that started everyone fighting. Austria–Hungary blamed Serbia and declared war on 28 July 1914. Russia went to war to help Serbia. Germany helped Austria–Hungary. Soon, France and Britain were fighting too.

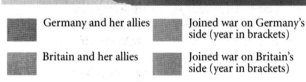

The alliance system in Europe in 1914.

Germany and her allies

Britain and her allies

Joined war on Germany's side (year in brackets)

Joined war on Britain's side (year in brackets)

A SOURCE

Crowds cheer the outbreak of war with Germany, 3 August 1914.
At this time, most people believed the war would be over by Christmas.

WHY DID MEN VOLUNTEER?

In two months, August and September 1914, three-quarters of a million British men **volunteered** to join the army. Why?

1. They believed that it was their duty to fight for their country – this is called **patriotism**.
2. The newspapers told them that the Germans were evil.
3. Some unemployed men joined up to get an army wage.

B SOURCE
Written by the historian Denis Winter in 1979.

Bert Warrant joined the army after robbing a cinema.
Private Jenkins joined up to get away from the police after stealing from German shops in London.
Men arrested in October 1914 for stealing from German shops were given a choice – join the army or go to prison.

C SOURCE
A government poster.

Come into the ranks and fight for your King and Country–Dont stay in the crowd and stare

YOU ARE WANTED AT · THE · FRONT
ENLIST TO·DAY

4. Men who volunteered together were allowed to fight together. Men from the same town joined 'Pals **battalions**'. It was hard to say 'No' when all your friends were joining up.
5. Girls loved a soldier's uniform!
6. If you didn't sign up, people called you a coward. Barmen in pubs would not serve you a beer. Women gave you white feathers. One poor chap, a war hero, escaped from a prisoner-of-war camp in Germany, walked home – and was given a white feather as soon as he got back because he was not in uniform!

All these reasons made it hard for men not to go to fight. One extra reason made it harder:

7. Everyone said the war would be over by Christmas – nobody in August 1914 knew how awful the First World War would be.

D SOURCE
An old man aged 103 remembers, 80 years later, why he joined up in 1913.

It was all very exciting. I was too young to understand about patriotism.

A lot of boys my age were joining up and I thought it would be like going on a picnic together. We all thought it would be over by Christmas.

Questions

a Use Source A and your own knowledge to explain why men volunteered for the army in the early years of the war.
b What does Source B tell us about the sort of men who volunteered to fight in 1914?
c How useful is Source C as evidence of the British public's reaction to the outbreak of war? Use Source C and your own knowledge to answer this question.
d Is Source D a fair interpretation of why men volunteered for the army in the First World War? Use Source D and your own knowledge to answer this question.

Key Issue

• Why did some men not want to fight?

Key Words
• conscription • Conscientious Objectors • Quakers • Socialists • Communists • businesses • shirkers • farm work • stretcher-bearers • prison • brave

As the war went on, fewer men **volunteered** to join the army. In September 1914 nearly half a million men had joined up. In December 1915 only 55,000 volunteered.

So, in 1916, the government brought in **conscription** – it told men aged 18–41 that they had to join the army, whether they wanted to or not. (Miners and shipyard workers did not have to join up.)

But some men refused. They said that the war was against their conscience (beliefs). They were called **Conscientious Objectors** (COs) – 16,000 men were listed as COs.

PACIFISTS AND SOCIALISTS

There are TWO main reasons that men became COs.

1. Some Christians (e.g. Quakers) believed it was wrong to kill anybody for any reason.
2. Some **Socialists** and **Communists** believed that the war was a plot by rich people to make more money, and they refused to kill their fellow workers, even if they were Germans.

Most COs agreed to do other work for the war effort. Some did farm work. Some became stretcher-bearers on the front line – many were very brave.

But some COs refused to help the war in any way. They were punished:

• They were put in prison.
• They were kept in prison after the war so that soldiers coming back from the war could get all the best jobs.
• They were not allowed to vote until 1926.

BUSINESS REASONS

Some men had other reasons for not wanting to go to war – they had a business to run. If they went to war, their business would go bankrupt. Some of these small businesses (for instance shopkeepers, shoemakers) were very important for the country and the war effort.

This Australian poster suggests that it is better and braver to be a soldier than a sportsman.

The government tried to help these people – four out of every five men who asked to stay out of the war were allowed to.

Not everybody who asked had a good reason not to fight. One man said that he could not join up because he had to take his wife a cup of tea in bed every morning!

SHIRKERS OR COWARDS?

Many people hated the COs. They said they were cowards or '**shirkers**' (lazy). They said that Britain was in a fight to the death, and that everyone ought to help or the country would be destroyed.

Many COs were attacked or abused.

A SOURCE

A Socialist song written by James Maxton, a British Socialist.
The 'Kaiser' was the ruler of Germany.

Oh, I'm Henry Dubb
And I won't go to war
Because I don't know
What they are all fighting for. . .

To Hell with the Kaiser
To Hell with the King

B SOURCE

This letter was written in September 1918 by a wine-shop owner trying to stop one of his workers – a man called Douglas Merry – being called up.

Mr Merry is my only worker left, as all the rest have been called up. He runs one of my shops instead of my son (who has also been called up) and he is the only worker I have who could do so. My shops pay lots of taxes and Mr Merry is not a very strong man. Please do not call him up.

*Since 1914 he has been a **Special Policeman** and he also does fire brigade work.*

C SOURCE

In this 1914 cartoon, the rich man is saying 'I must do something for the war – I'll get some more flags for the motorbike!'
Look at the man and the poster behind him – what is the message of the cartoon?

"GREAT SCOTT! I MUST DO SOMETHING. DASHED IF I DON'T GET SOME MORE FLAGS FOR THE OLD JIGGER!"

D SOURCE

A British soldier remembers what he thought about the COs.

I thought they were very brave – they had far more guts than all the people who were attacking them.

Questions

a What does Source A tell us about James Maxton's attitude to the war and the people in power?
b Use Source B and your own knowledge to explain why some men tried to avoid military service.
c How useful is Source C in explaining the attitude of the British people to men who didn't join up? Use Source C and your own knowledge to answer this question.
d Is Source D a fair interpretation of the attitude of people to Conscientious Objectors? Use Source D and your own knowledge to answer the question.

Key Issue

- How did the government try to control public opinion?

Key Words

- propaganda • lies • Lord Bryce • hate
- duty • censorship • newspapers • morale
- Church of England

PROPAGANDA

Propaganda is where a government publishes things to make people think what it wants them to think.

Some propaganda can be the truth – but sometimes propaganda is outright lies. In the First World War, the British government and newspapers made little effort to check if what they were saying was true.

THE BRYCE COMMISSION

Here is an example. In 1915, Lord Bryce published a report in 30 languages which made many people hate the Germans. Bryce claimed that – when they attacked Belgium – the German soldiers had:

1. Raped 20 girls in public.
2. Killed a young child (see Source C).
3. Cut the breasts off a girl.

Bryce said that his report was based on the words of 1200 Belgian people. But in fact he did not speak to a single person. In 1922 the Belgian government could not find one person who had seen any of these things.

Of course, when Germany attacked Belgium, 5000 Belgians were killed, but not in any of the ways Bryce said.

CENSORSHIP

Censorship is where a government stops you knowing things it does not want you to know.

Newspapers were censored during the war. The government said that bad news would be bad for **morale**. So when an Australian newspaperman told people how badly the fighting in Gallipoli (in Turkey) was going, he was sent to prison. The government had wanted to keep it quiet.

A SOURCE

A British poster claiming to show how Germans treated wounded British soldiers.

RED CROSS OR IRON CROSS?

WOUNDED AND A PRISONER
OUR SOLDIER CRIES FOR WATER.
THE GERMAN "SISTER"
POURS IT ON THE GROUND BEFORE HIS EYES.
THERE IS NO WOMAN IN BRITAIN
WHO WOULD DO IT.
THERE IS NO WOMAN IN BRITAIN
WHO WILL FORGET IT.

THE CHURCH

The Church of England told people it was right to fight. One vicar told people that the Germans planned to kill all the boys in Britain if they won the war. Christians who said you should love your enemies were attacked for undermining the war effort.

B SOURCE

This British poster tried to get people to lend money for the war effort by suggesting what Britain would be like if Germany won.

To prevent this –

F. GREGORY BROWN

BUY
WAR SAVINGS
CERTIFICATES
NOW

C SOURCE

One story from the Bryce Report, written as though reported by an eyewitness. (A **bayonet** is the knife soldiers attach to the end of their rifles.)

One day when the Germans were not bombing us, I went out to go to my mother's house in High Street.

I saw eight drunken German soldiers, singing and dancing in the street. A small child – I could not see if it was a boy or a girl – came into the street and got in their way.

The Germans were walking in twos. The first two went past the child, but one man in the second line pushed his bayonet into the child's belly. He lifted it into the air and carried it along on his bayonet – and he and his friends were still singing.

The child screamed when it was stabbed, but then it went quiet.

D SOURCE

Written by the historian M Gallo in 1989.

The British government tried to get men to join up by telling them it was their duty.

Questions

a What does Source A tell us about British propaganda methods?

b Use Source B and your own knowledge to explain what image of Germans British propaganda showed.

c How useful is Source C as evidence of German atrocities against civilians? Use Source C and your own knowledge to answer this question.

d Is Source D a fair interpretation of how the government tried to persuade men to enlist in the First World War? Use Source D and your own knowledge to answer this question.

Key Issue

- Germany had to fight a war on many fronts.

Key Words
1914: Western Front • war of movement • Marne • Eastern Front • Tannenberg
1915: stalemate • Second Battle of Ypres • Gallipoli • ANZACs • Italy
1916: attrition • Verdun • Somme • Brusilov • Jutland
1917: Passchendaele • Russian Revolution • America
1918: Operation Michael • Armistice

1914

WESTERN FRONT: THE WAR OF MOVEMENT

Everybody expected the war to be an exciting time of marches and cavalry charges. For a while in August and September 1914 the German army did advance quickly into Belgium and France. Historians call this 'the war of movement'. But on 5–10 September 1914 the French defeated the German army at the Battle of the Marne. Both sides dug trenches running from the sea to Switzerland (700 km).

The war of movement stopped and the war became a stalemate – a war of trenches, barbed wire, dug-outs and machine guns.

EASTERN FRONT

In the east, the Russian army invaded Germany, but the Russians were poorly-armed and badly-led. The German army killed tens of thousands of Russians at the Battle of Tannenberg (26–29 August 1914).

Turkey joined the war on the side of the Germans.

1915

WESTERN FRONT: STALEMATE

Neither side was able to break through the enemy's trenches. At the Second Battle of Ypres (April–May 1915), the Germans used poison gas, but they still could not break through.

EASTERN FRONT

Faced by the stalemate on the Western Front, the Germans concentrated on the Eastern Front, and the Russians were forced back.

GALLIPOLI

In Britain, faced by the stalemate on the Western Front, Winston Churchill persuaded the government to attack Turkey – but the troops who landed at Gallipoli were defeated, losing thousands of men.

THE ITALIAN FRONT

Italy joined the war on the side of Britain and France, and attacked Austria.

1916

WESTERN FRONT: THE WAR OF ATTRITION

The Germans now tried to win the war by a 'war of **attrition**' – they decided to fight, whatever the losses, until their enemies were 'worn down'. So 1916 saw two of the biggest battles of the war – the Battles of Verdun (February–December 1916: 300,000 men died) and the Somme (July–November 1916: 400,000 men died). The Somme was the battle where the British first used tanks.

THE EASTERN FRONT

The Russian general Brusilov attacked the Austrians and drove them back – the Germans had to send soldiers to help them.

THE WAR AT SEA

The German and the British navies fought the Battle of Jutland – the most important battle of 1916 because the British navy stopped food getting to Germany.

1917

THE WESTERN FRONT

The war of attrition continued. In August–November 1917 the British attacked the Germans at the Battle of Passchendaele: 600,000 men died.

THE EASTERN FRONT

In 1917 there was a revolution in Russia. The new **Communist** government made peace with the Germans and pulled out of the war. This meant that Germany could now concentrate on the Western Front.

AMERICA ENTERS THE WAR

In 1917, however, America came into the war on the side of Britain and France. American troops began to come to Europe at the rate of 250,000 a month.

The First World War. See how Germany had to fight on many different 'fronts'.

1918

WESTERN FRONT: GERMANY DEFEATED

Germany was tired. Back home, Germans were living on potatoes and berries.

So the Germans tried to win the war before too many American soldiers arrived. They made a huge last attack called 'Operation Michael', breaking through at certain points and then driving hard into France. They got to just 80 km from Paris. For a time, it looked as if they might win the war.

But then the British, French and Americans stopped the German advance and drove them back.

British troops rest in their dug-outs.

Turkey surrendered in October, then Austria (4 November). Germany's last effort had failed, and the war was lost. On 11 November 1918, Germany agreed to a ceasefire (the **'Armistice'**).

Questions

a What was the battle in 1914 that halted the German advance into France?
b Why was this defeat a serious one for the Germans?
c How does the map show the difficulties Germany faced during the war?
d What impact did Russia's surrender have on the war?

Controversy!

'When you look at what happened in the First World War, it is clear that – from beginning to end – nobody had a clue what they were doing. The great powers just made it up as they went along.'

What is your INSTANT REACTION?

5 THE SCHLIEFFEN PLAN

Key Issue

> Why did the Schlieffen Plan fail?

Key Words
- Schlieffen • war on two fronts • Alsace–Lorraine • 90% • food and ammunition • Moltke • BEF • Mons • Marne

In 1914 Germany was ready for war. A German general called Alfred von Schlieffen had started preparing for it in 1892!

In 1905 he finished his plan – 'the Schlieffen Plan'. It was a good plan and, if it had succeeded, Germany would have won the war.

THE PLAN IN DETAIL

Schlieffen's main problem was that Germany was going to have to fight France on one side and Russia on the other. This is called a 'war on two fronts' and it is very dangerous.

Schlieffen's answer was that he was going to try to beat France very quickly, and then get his armies back across Germany to fight Russia before the Russians had got ready.

Schlieffen's plan to beat France was this:

1. He knew that the French wanted to get back Alsace–Lorraine.
2. He kept the German army there very small, so that it would tempt the French to make their main attack there.
3. He kept 90% of the German army in the north. When the French attacked, this force would sweep down into France and capture Paris (and then rush back to face the Russians).

However, Schlieffen's Plan needed three things:

- The army in the north had to be huge – 90% of the whole army.
- The German soldiers had to march 35 kilometres a day, and the army had to supply them with food and ammunition.

Artillery (big guns) killed more men than any other weapon in the war.

- Russia had to take three months to get ready for war.

Schlieffen died in 1913 and a general called Moltke took over.

THE OUTCOME

Moltke attacked France on 4 August 1914. But the Schlieffen Plan failed:

1. Moltke got worried, and sent more troops than he needed to Alsace–Lorraine.
2. Russia took only six weeks to get ready, not twelve, and Moltke had to send 100,000 men to Russia – so his northern army was only 60% of his men, not 90%.
3. The German army did not supply enough food or ammunition for the soldiers, who got very tired.
4. The British sent the British Expeditionary Force (BEF) to fight the Germans. It was only 75,000 men, but it held up the German army at the Battle of Mons (23 August 1914) and gave the French time to set up defences at the River Marne ready for the German attack.
5. At the Battle of the Marne (5–10 September 1914), just 60 km from Paris, the French and British stopped the Germans and drove them back.

Moltke told the German Emperor Wilhelm: 'We have lost the war'. He was sacked.

STALEMATE

The Germans fell back a little, then they dug a trench. When the French attacked, the Germans killed them with machine guns. So the French dug a trench too. Before long, both sides had a system of trenches stretching from Switzerland to the sea, and that was how the war went on for the next four years.

A SOURCE

The Battle of Mons – an account written by two historians, J Winter and B Baggett, in 1996.

The British were attacked by wave after wave of Germans, marching across the open fields. Lots of German soldiers were shot, but the Germans generals thought it was worth it to keep moving quickly. But there were too few British soldiers to stop the German army altogether, and they were in danger of being surrounded.

B SOURCE

A British soldier remembers the Battle of Mons, 60 years afterwards.

They sent us to a field and told us to dig in. So we dug a hole and waited. The party started when the Germans came. There were thousands of them, and we just shot them down.

But they still kept coming. In the end there were enough of them to shove us out of the field.

C SOURCE

An account of the battle written by the historian Trevor Wilson in 1986.

By the end of the day's fighting, the British found that they had held up the Germans, but the French hadn't done their bit. In fact, without telling the BEF, the French had fallen back, and the British were in danger of finding themselves alone.

So they had to retreat, and fight their way back to safety.

This British machine gun could fire 500 bullets a minute – as many as 60 ordinary riflemen.

E SOURCE

Map of the Schlieffen Plan.

The march into France.

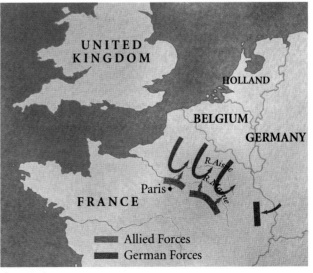

The Allied counter-attack.

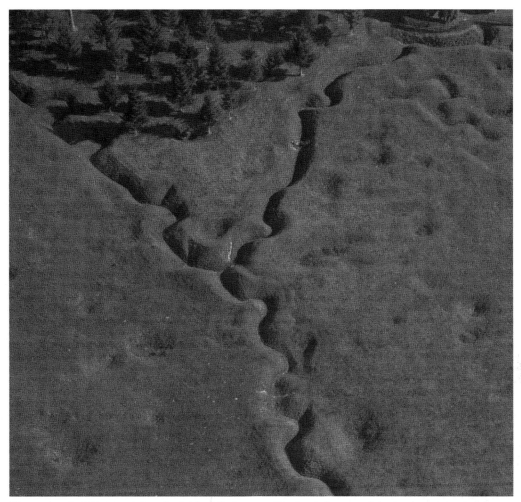

The remains of a British trench from the Battle of the Somme. Note how it zig-zags. Note also the remains of shell-craters all around.

F SOURCE

A comment by the historians J Winter and B Baggett in 1996.

The Russian soldiers were nowhere near as good as the Germans, but there were millions of them. So the Germans had to send soldiers to fight Russia, and in this way Russia saved the French in 1914.

1. Copy, in what you believe is their order of importance, the five reasons why the Schlieffen Plan failed.
2. Write down and explain three reasons why the British lost the Battle of Mons.

Controversy!

'Germany should have surrendered in September 1914, when the Schlieffen Plan failed – they had lost the war.'

What is your INSTANT REACTION?

Questions

a What can you learn from Source A about the Battle of Mons?
b Does Source C support the evidence of Sources A and B about the Battle of Mons?
c How useful are Sources D and F as evidence of the reasons for the failure of the Schlieffen Plan?
d 'The Schlieffen Plan failed because of the British role at the Battle of Mons.' Use the sources, and your own knowledge, to explain whether you agree with this view.

Key Issue

• Why was there a stalemate on the Western Front?

After the brief 'war of movement' in August–September 1914, both sides dug trenches. Each side built at least three lines of trenches:

• A front trench

• A support trench

• A reserve trench

The trenches had up to 30 metres of barbed wire to defend them. They were linked by more trenches so that if the front line trench was attacked, more soldiers could be sent to defend it. Trenches were also zig-zagged so that even if the enemy succeeded in reaching the trench, they would only capture a single bay.

The trenches made it almost impossible for an army to advance. The war became a **stalemate**, where neither side could break through the enemy's lines.

NO MAN'S LAND

The land between the two lines of trenches (which was in some places only 100 metres wide) was called No Man's Land. Both sides dug short trenches (called **saps**) into No Man's Land to listen out for enemy attacks at night.

To capture an enemy trench, soldiers had to go 'over the top' (get out of their own trench) and cross No Man's Land.

Before an attack, both sides would shell the enemy trenches with a huge **artillery** bombardment. During these bombardments, soldiers would hide in underground dug-outs. The German dug-outs were very deep and well-built (sometimes 15 metres below ground, with thick concrete walls).

The trenches of the Great War were supposed to look like this. Sandbags protect the front and the rear of the trench. Note the four different parts of the trench (labelled). Each part had a purpose – can you think what?

MINING OPERATIONS

Both sides dug long tunnels under enemy lines, packed them with dynamite, and set them off just before their men went over the top to attack the enemy trenches. The huge explosion was supposed to kill and confuse the enemy, and open up a gap in the enemy trench system.

Key Words

• trenches • barbed wire • bays • stalemate • No Man's Land • 'over the top' • the Somme • machine guns • artillery • firing step • mines • craters • creeping barrage • General Haig

The British began the Battle of Passchendaele by exploding 19 **mines**. Two did not explode and were forgotten in the battle – one went off in 1955 during a storm; the other is still out there today, waiting to explode by accident.

Mines blew huge **craters** in the ground which are still there today. But they were not enough to help the soldiers to break through the enemy lines.

PREPARATIONS FOR BATTLE

The generals on both sides had no idea how to break through and end the stalemate. In the end, all they could think of was to make huge attacks to try to wear down the enemy.

Before an attack, large numbers of men would be taken to the line. Millions of shells and bullets, with food and other supplies, would be sent there too. Lots of coffins would be dumped by the roadside.

Of course, enemy planes could see all this happening days before the attack was made, and the enemy soldiers would get ready for the attack.

ARTILLERY BOMBARDMENTS

Most attacks started with an artillery bombardment. Before the Battle of the Somme (1916), the British guns fired 1.5 million shells on the Germans. The generals told the men that the shells would kill the defenders and destroy the German trenches and barbed wire. They were telling lies – after a week's bombardment, a British report said: 'The German dug-outs are good and the German soldiers are safe'.

What the bombardment had done, of course, was warn the Germans that an attack was coming soon.

Usually the bombardment stopped just before the men went over the top, giving the enemy time to get to his firing-steps to machine-gun the soldiers as they advanced across No Man's Land.

Sometimes, however, the artillery set up a **'creeping barrage'**, firing their shells just ahead of the men as they advanced. The problem with this was that, sometimes, the shells fell short and killed their own men.

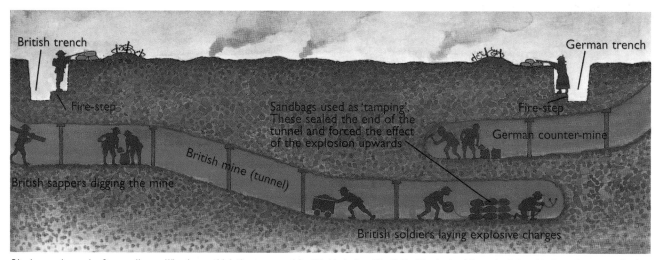

British trench   German trench

Fire-step

Sandbags used as 'tamping'. These sealed the end of the tunnel and forced the effect of the explosion upwards

Fire-step

German counter-mine

British sappers digging the mine

British mine (tunnel)

British soldiers laying explosive charges

Digging a mine under German lines. Who do you think the army used for this kind of work? Both sides had soldiers who listened to hear the enemy digging mines. If they did, they would dig their own tunnel into the enemy mine, and soldiers would crawl to fight to the death in the dark and the mud under No Man's Land.

'OVER THE TOP'

Before an attack, soldiers had to cut pathways through their own barbed wire so that the men going over the top could get through. When the attack came, the enemy machine guns simply killed the men as they walked down these pathways in single file.

Going over the top was a race – you had to get to the enemy lines before the enemy could set up his machine-guns and start firing. Yet at the Battle of the Somme, British soldiers were told to walk across No Man's Land so that they would not get separated from their units.

A SOURCE

A photo from the Battle of Passchendaele, 1917. British stretcher-bearers carry a wounded man. Notice the gas mask bags and Red Cross armbands.

THE STRATEGY OF THE GENERALS

Month after month, the generals just kept sending more and more men over the top to their deaths. It is easy to understand why many soldiers hated the generals.

General Haig was head of the British Army from 1915 until the end of the war. Many historians have said that he was a stupid man for using tactics which killed so many men. But other historians have defended him saying:

- He kept the British army fighting in 1917, when both the French and the Russian armies gave up.
- What else could he do? He did not have modern technology to win the war.
- He *did* use new inventions whenever he could, e.g. tanks, gas, cars, and planes.
- He won in the end.

A typical trench system on the Western Front.

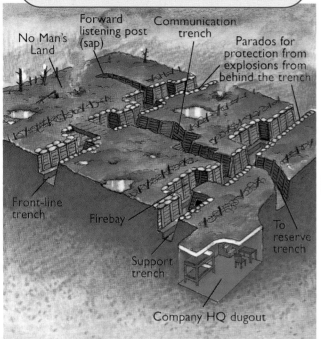

No Man's Land

Forward listening post (sap)

Communication trench

Parados for protection from explosions from behind the trench

Front-line trench

Firebay

To reserve trench

Support trench

Company HQ dugout

A soldier remembers in the 1970s what he thought of the generals.

I hated the generals who made us live in the dirt, and then sent us to die, just so that they would look good.

Controversy!

'Historians talk about the trench system as though it was a failure.   They couldn't be more wrong!   Given the technology of the time, it was the best-planned, most brilliantly-executed system of defence the world has ever seen.   Historians are always criticising the generals because they couldn't 'break through' – why don't they praise them for devising the trench system?'
What is your INSTANT REACTION?

What the modern historian John Laffin thinks of General Haig.

Haig simply thought that if he killed more Germans than the Germans could kill of his men, then he would win in the end.

The generals had no real strategy at all. It was just slaughter.

Questions

a What does Source A tell you about how the weather affected the fighting on the Western Front?
b Use Source B and your own knowledge to explain why these trenches were so difficult to capture.
c How useful is Source C as evidence of the attitude of British soldiers towards their generals?   Use Source C and your own knowledge to answer this question.
d 'The generals had no real strategy at all.   It was just slaughter.'   Is this a fair interpretation of the role of British commanders during the war?   Use Source D and your own knowledge to answer this question.

1. Read pages 14–17 and find eight reasons why it was impossible to break through an enemy trench.
2. Discuss this as a class and list them in order of importance.

7 LIFE IN THE TRENCHES

Key Issue

- What was life like in the trenches?

Key Words
- fatigues • danger • trench foot • duckboards • 'Blighty one' • latrines • lice • 'bung' • 'barkers' • Christmas truce • 'in cold blood'

Life in a World War One trench was mainly boring.

Most of a soldier's time was spent doing '**fatigues**' – work such as repairing the barbed wire, pumping out flooded trenches, and emptying latrines (toilets). In a month, a soldier might spend eight days in the front line, eight days in the reserve trench, and the rest of the time in a local town away from the fighting.

If there was a big attack, however, all that could change. Then a soldier might have to spend up to six weeks in the front line, and living conditions became very dirty and nasty, as well as dangerous.

TRENCH FOOT

When soldiers spent a lot of time standing in water they got 'trench foot' – their feet swelled, turned black, and in the end their toes and even feet had to be cut off. To try to stop this, men put 'duckboards' along the bottom of the trench. They were also supposed to put on dry socks and to rub whale oil into their feet to stop themselves getting trench foot.

Some soldiers tried to get trench foot *on purpose* – it was a way of getting 'a **Blighty** one', a wound that did not kill you, but was bad enough to get you sent home to 'Blighty' (Britain).

HYGIENE

Trenches were dirty and unhealthy.

Latrines were just pits dug in the ground off a **sap** in No Man's Land. They were smelly, unhealthy – and dangerous, because the enemy would lob a shell into them from time to time, just to catch anyone who might be sitting there!

Another big problem was lice. Their bites itched and led to boils and trench fever. Soldiers would run candle flames along the seams of their clothes to try to pop the eggs, but nothing could get rid of them altogether.

Food in the trenches was awful too. Cheese was known as 'bung' because it gave you constipation, and army sausages were called 'barkers' because the soldiers said they were made of dog meat.

THE CHRISTMAS TRUCE, 1914

At Christmas 1914, the soldiers on both sides left their trenches and swapped food and cigarettes. It is said that at one place they even had a game of football. The spirit of Christmas overcame the hatreds of war.

The generals were angry when they heard this. They thought that the men would find it harder to kill the Germans if they had met them. They moved the men who had taken part in the Christmas truce to different parts of the line, and they forbade them ever to do anything like that again.

A SOURCE

An account of the Christmas truce written by the British general, Sir John French.

I am told that unarmed German soldiers ran over to our trenches carrying Christmas trees, and that some of our men were friendly to them.

When I heard that this had happened, I stopped it.

B SOURCE

Christmas in No Man's Land.

C SOURCE

A British soldier remembers why one truce had to be delayed.

At lunchtime, the Germans sent a message to say that their general was visiting the line that afternoon, so we'd better keep our heads down – they would have to do a little shooting to make things look right for him.

E SOURCE

A fight in the trenches, remembered by a soldier 60 years after the war.

Some of the Germans put up a good fight, but some begged us on their knees, holding up photos of wives and children. We killed them all in cold blood because it was our duty to kill as many as we could. I remembered all those men, women and children the Germans had killed. I had prayed for that day, and when it happened, I killed as many as I could.

D SOURCE

Both sides cared for wounded enemy soldiers. Here, a British soldier gives a wounded German a drink.

F SOURCE

Many years later, a soldier remembers how the generals stopped a Christmas truce.

The generals must have found out something was going on, because they ordered the artillery to attack the German lines. That started the fighting again. We were cursing the generals to hell.

Under the title 'What was life like in the trenches?', write a sentence about each of the following:
fatigues, dangerous, trench foot, latrines, lice, food, Christmas truce.

Questions

a What can you learn from Source A about the Christmas truce of 1914?

b Does Source C support the evidence of Sources A and B about truces between British and German soldiers?

d Study Sources D and E. How useful are these two sources as evidence of British feelings towards Germans on the Western Front?

d 'The ordinary British soldier had no real desire to fight Germans.' Use the sources and your own knowledge to explain whether you agree with this view.

Key Issue

→ What was it like to fight in a battle in the First World War?

Key Words

- duty • coward • dug-out • frightened
- 'copping a Blighty' • training • shrapnel
- buried bodies • mud • wounded
- army doctors • blood-poisoning

Most soldiers did not want to go into battle, but they knew it was their duty to go over the top. Many of them felt they could not let down their fellow soldiers. Many of them also did not want to look like a coward.

This photo is of a German dug-out. This dug-out was captured by the British in 1917, but was then forgotten. It was recently discovered by accident.
The dug-out is made of thick concrete. It held 36 men and four officers. The men slept two to a bunk, except the officers, who had a bunk each.

'COPPING A BLIGHTY'

A soldier who 'copped a **Blighty** one' would be sent back home, but soldiers hated a man who gave himself a wound so that he could get away from the fighting. This was seen as a coward's way out, and men who did this on purpose were shot.

When 18-year-old Eric Hiscock accidentally wounded himself in the arm while cleaning his rifle, his officer was very angry (see Source A, page 22). Hiscock was lucky. He did not get shot, but he was fined ten days' pay.

WAITING TO ATTACK

Before an attack, many soldiers were frightened – they knew there was a good chance they were going to die. Once the attack started, many soldiers said that their training took over and they forgot their fear. The waiting was the worst part.

60 years afterwards, a soldier remembered waiting the night before an attack:

> I didn't get a wink of sleep that night. What were my chances? A quarter of us would not get hurt at all. But a third would probably be killed, and another quarter wounded. Some of us would be taken prisoner – as good as getting off without being hurt.

THE TERROR OF BATTLE

Artillery shells killed more soldiers than any other cause in the First World War. The shells exploded a few metres above the ground, and red-hot bits of **shrapnel** flew into the bodies of any soldiers nearby.

Sometimes there was nothing left of a soldier who had been hit by a shell. Many soldiers were killed, but their bodies were never found – they were blown to pieces, buried in shell holes and drowned in the mud.

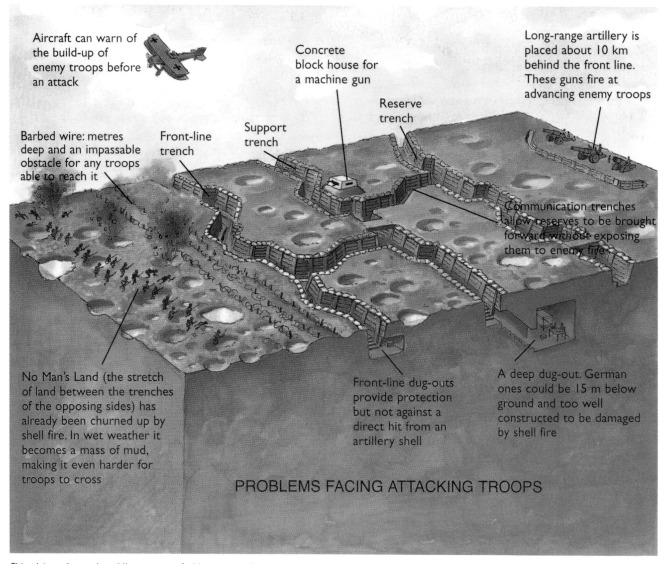

Aircraft can warn of the build-up of enemy troops before an attack

Concrete block house for a machine gun

Long-range artillery is placed about 10 km behind the front line. These guns fire at advancing enemy troops

Reserve trench

Support trench

Barbed wire: metres deep and an impassable obstacle for any troops able to reach it

Front-line trench

Communication trenches allow reserves to be brought forward without exposing them to enemy fire

No Man's Land (the stretch of land between the trenches of the opposing sides) has already been churned up by shell fire. In wet weather it becomes a mass of mud, making it even harder for troops to cross

Front-line dug-outs provide protection but not against a direct hit from an artillery shell

A deep dug-out. German ones could be 15 m below ground and too well constructed to be damaged by shell fire

PROBLEMS FACING ATTACKING TROOPS

This picture shows why soldiers were so afraid to go over the top.

When the shell exploded, hundreds of iron balls and jagged fragments of the shell casing were driven down on the attacking troops

a   b   c   d

A typical shrapnel shell
a   Bursting charge
b   Bullets
c   Flash tube from fuze
d   Fuze

An artillery shell exploding.

Dead soldiers were buried quickly, so that there was less chance of disease. If they were lucky, they were remembered and re-buried later in the proper cemeteries, but many were forgotten and left. Sometimes shell-fire blew up buried bodies, and a World War One battlefield was often a mess of slime, bones and rotting bits of flesh.

80 years afterwards, a man remembers burying dead bodies:

> When you lifted a body, the arms and legs were pulled off from the body. The bodies crawled with maggots. Every now and then we had to stop to be sick. Once, I fell and my hand went through the belly of a dead man. My hand smelled of it for months.

AN EXPERIENCE OF PASSCHENDAELE

In 1917, heavy rain flooded the battlefield of Passchendaele adding another danger – drowning in the mud – to the lives of the men.

Seventy years later, Captain Vaughan remembers getting trapped in the mud:

> I only stopped for a moment in the shell-hole, but I felt myself sinking into the mud. I saw the leg of a dead body sticking out of the side but, when I grabbed at it, it just came off in my hand. I pulled in a couple of rifles and yelled for the troops to throw me more.

Captain Vaughan got out of the mud, but 75 of the 90 men he had led into the attack were killed or wounded.

Controversy!
'Never in the history of the world have human beings voluntarily put themselves through such hell as a World War One battle. Nothing before or after has ever been as bad.'

What is your INSTANT REACTION?

THE WOUNDED

To be wounded in the First World War was a terrible thing. You were given first aid on the battlefield, and then taken behind the lines.

The army doctors worked tirelessly to save the men's lives, and were amongst the bravest men of the war.

But the problem was blood-poisoning. Dirt got into the wound, and the wound became infected. Modern medicines had not yet been invented, and many men died because their wounds became infected. In all, 8 out of every 100 wounded men died of their wounds. Head wounds were the worst – half the men who had head wounds died from their wounds.

A SOURCE
Hiscock remembers how he was punished for wounding himself.

'Hiscock – you are under arrest. You'll probably be shot for this!' said the officer. He was right. I had shot myself, though I knew it had been an accident.

'Shot himself' was one of the most shameful wounds of the war.

B SOURCE
A soldier remembers why he kept fighting.

They say you get used to death, but I don't think we ever did. We were very sad when a man died, but we had happy times as well, and there was a sense of friendship you will never understand if you were not there. We would have done anything to help one of our friends.

A photo of cheering British troops on their way to the Battle of the Somme, 1916.

D **SOURCE**

A cigarette advert from the war.

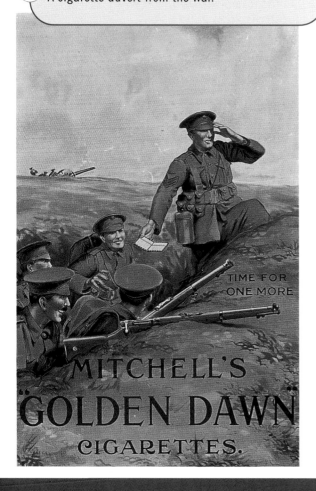

TIME FOR ONE MORE

MITCHELL'S "GOLDEN DAWN" CIGARETTES.

Questions

a What does Source A tell you about the army's attitude to men who shot themselves to get out of the fighting?

b Use Source B and your own knowledge to explain why men continued to fight, despite the horror and dangers.

c How useful is Source C as evidence of the attitude of British soldiers to the war? Use Source C and your own knowledge to answer this question.

d Is Source D a fair interpretation of how soldiers went into battle? Use Source D and your own knowledge to answer this question.

Controversy!

'The worst thing about the soldiers' experience of battle was the difference between what they had expected it to be like, and what it actually turned out like.'
What is your INSTANT REACTION?

9 GALLIPOLI

Key Issue

→ Why was the Gallipoli campaign a failure?

Key Words

• stalemate • 'weak point' • Winston Churchill • navy • Gallipoli • ANZAC beach • Turks • hills • Suvla Bay • 'war of attrition'

By 1915, the war on the Western Front had ground to a **stalemate**. So both sides tried to find a 'weak point' by opening up new fronts elsewhere in the world.

In 1915, therefore, Winston Churchill (who had been put in charge of the navy) persuaded the British government to attack Gallipoli in Turkey. Churchill hoped that, if he defeated Turkey, he would be able to help Russia. He hoped this would help to break the stalemate on the Western Front.

But the attack on Gallipoli was a disaster.

ANZAC LANDINGS

First, Churchill ordered an attack by the British navy in March 1915. Not only did this fail – three battleships were sunk by Turkish **mines** – but it gave the Turks a month's warning where the attack was going to take place.

When the British and ANZAC (Australian and New Zealand) troops landed in April 1915, the Turks were ready for them. The attackers were trapped on the beaches as the Turks fired down on them from the hills all around. 150,000 men were killed in the next 9 months, before Churchill eventually gave up the attack.

Churchill resigned and went to fight on the Western Front.

FAILURE OF THE 'WEAK POINT' STRATEGY

Gallipoli had proved that there was no such thing as a 'weak point'.

But it also convinced the government that there was no other way to win the war than to fight to the death on the Western Front. At the same time, the Germans were deciding the same thing. So Gallipoli was the start of the 'war of **attrition**' of 1916–17, where both sides just set about attacking each other, whatever the losses, until one of them was worn down and forced to surrender.

A SOURCE

Written in an encyclopaedia (1998).

In April 1915, 78,000 troops landed on the Gallipoli beaches. They were faced with high cliffs and they were too far apart to help each other. Another landing was made in August at Suvla Bay. This time, there were no Turkish troops to fight them, but the generals wasted time until the Turkish army had got ready, and another stalemate followed.

B SOURCE

Written by Major Farmar, a British soldier, in 1915.

The generals did not plan their attacks carefully enough.

They did not listen to the ordinary soldiers, and they used tired men from the trenches, not fresh troops, to attack.

The Turks were in strong positions.

C SOURCE

A soldier remembers the battle at Suvla.

We landed at Suvla beach, but no one told us to attack. So we waited, while the Turks sent more and more soldiers to defend the cliffs.

When we attacked, very many of our men were killed.

My officer said to me: 'Tell the General that many men are being killed'.

I ran down the hill and told the General, who looked at me as if to say: 'We have only been fighting for three hours – how can this be true?'

Then, however, another runner came to say that 75% of his men had been killed. I remember the General looking up and saying: 'My God, it must be true'.

D SOURCE

Anzac Beach, painted by an Australian.

E SOURCE

The Gallipoli campaign, 1915.

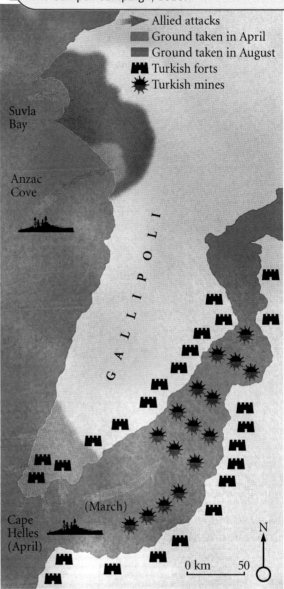

Allied attacks
Ground taken in April
Ground taken in August
Turkish forts
Turkish mines

Suvla Bay

Anzac Cove

GALLIPOLI

(March)

Cape Helles (April)

N

0 km   50

F SOURCE

An Australian soldier, talking in the 1970s about the Gallipoli campaign.

Me and all the men respected the Turkish soldiers.

They were fair fighters and very brave. They were not frightened by heavy fire, and nothing would stop them.

Questions

a What can you learn from Source A about the Gallipoli campaign?
b Does Source C support the evidence of Sources A and B about the way the campaign was carried out by the Allied commanders?
c How useful are Sources D and E as evidence about the Gallipoli campaign?
d 'The Gallipoli campaign failed because of bad planning.' Use the sources and your own knowledge to explain whether you agree with this view.

Key Issue

→ Why was the British attack a failure?

Key Words
• 'lions led by donkeys' • Verdun • 420,000 British, 650,000 Germans killed or wounded • was Haig a good general? • cavalry • tank • rush • walk • 'muddy grave of the German army'

One German general said that the British soldiers were 'lions led by donkeys'.

What do you think he meant when he called the British soldiers 'lions'?

And what do you think he meant when he called the British generals 'donkeys'?

When the Battle of the Somme was planned the Germans were attacking the French at Verdun. The idea was to help the French at Verdun by attacking the Germans at the Somme.

But it meant that most of the fighting would have to be done by the British soldiers.

GERMANY'S 'MUDDY GRAVE'

The first day of the Battle of the Somme – 1 July 1916 – was a disaster for the British soldiers. Half of them were killed or wounded – 20,000 killed and 40,000 wounded, most of them in the first hour as they went 'over the top' to walk towards the German machine guns.

But the first day of the Somme was not the end of the slaughter. Haig carried on the attacks until November, by which time 420,000 British and 195,000 French soldiers had been killed or wounded.

Many historians have said that Haig was a stupid general.

They say:

• Why did he keep sending men to their death when there was no chance of breaking through?

• Haig did not understand how important machine guns were – he did not think that the British army needed them. He said that cavalry soldiers were better!

• Haig *did* use the new secret weapon – the tank – but only 49 of them!

But some historians defend Haig. It was not his fault that the shells were so badly made that a third of them failed to explode. And, in the end, the battle *did* harm the German army. 650,000 Germans were killed or wounded, and one German called the battle 'the muddy grave of the German army'.

WERE THERE ALTERNATIVES?

The historian John Laffin says that Haig was a bad general. He says that Haig should have let the Germans attack, so he could have killed them and not lost so many of his own men.

Another historian, Paul Fussell, has pointed out that Haig ignored some good ideas. Two minutes before an attack, the British guns stopped firing. This was so they wouldn't kill their own men, but it warned the Germans that an attack was coming – which gave them time to get to their machine guns. One officer suggested that the artillery should stop, wait a while, then start again – so it could kill all the Germans who had rushed to their posts! But Haig never tried the idea.

TO RUSH OR NOT TO RUSH?

Another good idea that Haig ignored was the French way of attacking. Instead of going over the top in a huge mob and being shot by machine guns, the French rushed forward in small groups, hiding in shell holes for cover.

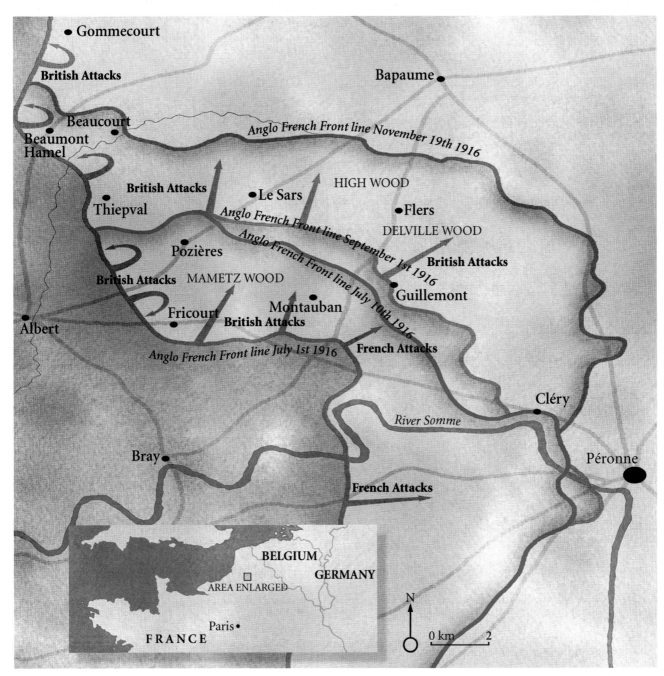

This map shows that the British army captured 13 kilometres of ground.   Was it worth the 620,000 British and French soldiers killed or wounded?

The French did this at the Battle of the Somme, and they lost fewer men and captured more ground than the British.

Haig never tried this idea.   He said that the British guns had killed all the Germans, and that the attack would be easy.   Also, the British troops were mostly young, new soldiers and Haig did not think they could attack like the French.   So Haig told the British troops to walk across No Man's Land in long lines – and the German machine-gunners easily mowed them down in their thousands.

A SOURCE

An account written by the historian M Middlebrook in 1971.

After three or four days of shelling, the German barbed wire was destroyed in some places, but in other places it was untouched.
Meanwhile, the British had cut pathways in their own barbed wire so the soldiers could attack.   The German machine-gunners turned their guns on these narrow pathways that were death-traps.

C SOURCE

An account written by the historian Nigel Jones in 1983.

The vast shell bombardment did not cut the German barbed wire, and it did not destroy the deep German dug-out and trenches.

The British generals did not realise how strong the German defences were and this, and the order to walk across No Man's Land, were the two main reasons for the failure of the attack.

Controversy!

'We who live in a world of smart bombs and satellite systems, have no right to judge in retrospect First World War generals who had only men with rifles.   Haig won in the end – what more do you want?'

What is your INSTANT REACTION?

D SOURCE

A British **mine** exploding before the attack on 1 July 1916. It exploded ten minutes too soon, giving the Germans ten minutes to get ready.

F SOURCE

A comment by the historian John Ellis in 1976.

The British made the Germans' job easy. They cut pathways in their own barbed wire so their men could attack. As one soldier said: 'It was like putting a sign up where we were going to attack, and that was why the German machine guns were so deadly'.

E SOURCE

An account written by a British soldier on 4 July 1916.

Our bombardment had greatly damaged the German trenches, which were mostly completely knocked in. But it hadn't destroyed the deep German dug-outs, so it hadn't knocked out the Germans machine guns.

Our shells had completely destroyed the enemy barbed wire.

Controversy!

'It is a sad comment on the British generals, but Britain won the war simply because they were more prepared than the Germans to see their soldiers slaughtered.'

What is your INSTANT REACTION?

Questions

a What can you learn from Source A about the British artillery bombardment at the start of the Battle of the Somme?
b Does Source C support the evidence of Sources A and B about the British attack?
c How useful are Sources D and E as evidence of the effectiveness of the British attack?
d 'The British offensive on the Somme was a failure because the attack was badly planned.' Using the sources and your own knowledge, explain whether you agree with this view.

Key Issue

- Why was Russia defeated?

Key Words

- Eastern Front • Russians • Tannenberg
- Schlieffen Plan • Tsar Nicholas • Brusilov
- Austria • (Verdun and the Somme)
- morale • Communist revolution

When is a defeat not a defeat? In 1914 the Russians invaded Germany. At the Battle of Tannenberg (August 1914), 30,000 Russians were killed or wounded, and 95,000 were taken prisoner. It was a huge defeat.

But the Russian attack was important because it forced the Germans to send troops from the Western Front to fight the Russians in the east, and this was vital in helping the French to defeat the Schlieffen Plan (see Chapter 5).

RUSSIAN SUCCESS

In 1915, the ruler of Russia, Tsar Nicholas, took over as head of the army, but the defeats went on. By the end of 1915, a million Russian soldiers had been killed.

Nevertheless, in June 1916, the Russian general Brusilov attacked the Austrians. He advanced quickly into Austria, and took 70,000 prisoners in a week. To stop him, the Germans had to take more troops from the Western Front. Many Russian soldiers were killed, and the attack came to a halt in October, but the Russians had been a great help:

- They helped the British and French in the battles of Verdun and the Somme, because the Germans had to send troops from the Western Front to help Austria.
- They greatly defeated the Austrians, who lost heart and were no help to the Germans for the rest of the war.

REVOLUTION

The cost to Russia, however, was great. People blamed Tsar Nicholas for the failures and hardships of the war. In 1917 there was a revolution in Russia and Nicholas gave up the throne.

At first, the new government tried to carry on the war, but in November 1917 it too fell from power. A **Communist** government under Lenin took over, and Russia pulled out of the war.

The Germans were now able to move all their troops from the Eastern Front to try to win the war on the Western Front.

WHY WAS RUSSIA DEFEATED?

Russia was defeated for four reasons:

1. The Russian army was badly-equipped and badly-led.
2. The Eastern Front was huge – 1800 km long – and almost impossible to defend.
3. The war ruined Russia, and people did not have food or fuel. In the end, they rebelled and a Communist government came to power which promised to end the war.
4. So many soldiers were killed that they came to hate the Tsar, and would not defend him when there was a revolution.

However, the Russians, in 1914 and 1916, were a great help to the British and French at vital moments in the war.

A SOURCE

A British woman remembers an event that happened when she was a nurse in Russia.

A young soldier came to us. He was sad and angry about the war, and he blamed the generals.

'They do not know how tired we are' he said. 'They sit in their hotels far from the fighting, and say: "We will capture that town in three days". And our men – hungry, cold and tired to death – have to go and fight, no matter how many of them are killed.'

B SOURCE

1917: German and Russian soldiers hear that Russia has pulled out of the war (the Russians are wearing fur hats).

Zensiert.
Paul Hoffmann & Co.
Berlin-Schöneberg.

Waffenruhe an der Ostfront. Beim Tauschhandel.

1802.

C SOURCE

A Russian soldier writes about the state of the Russian Army in 1917.

I didn't want to fight after Tsar Nicholas gave up the throne. The people who were supposed to send us food and weapons ran away.

We were hungry. We were dirty. Nobody obeyed orders. In the end, we ran away too.

D SOURCE

A Russian general writes about the state of the Russian Army in April 1917.

Things are getting worse every day and the army is falling apart.

1. Soldiers are running away.

2. They will not obey their officers.

3. The officers have given up hope.

4. Everybody wants peace.

5. Propaganda against the war is everywhere.

E SOURCE

A Russian poster of 1915 trying to get Russians to support the war. The Russian knight is cutting off the heads of Austria, Germany and Turkey.

Can you see in the background all the towns the Germans have destroyed?

Questions

a What can you learn from Source A about the **morale** of the Russian army during the war?

b Does Source C support the evidence of Sources A and B about the morale of the Russian army during the war?

c How useful are Sources D and E as evidence of Russian attitudes to the war?

d 'The Russian army collapsed because of poor leadership.' Using the sources and your own knowledge, explain whether you agree with this view.

Key Issue

How did poison gas affect the fighting?

Key Words
• defenders' advantage • chlorine • phosgene • mustard gas • blinded • urine • fires • gas masks • John Sargent • Loos

In the First World War, defenders with machine guns easily killed the attackers running across No Man's Land with rifles. In April 1915, therefore, the Germans used a new weapon they hoped would help the attackers – poison gas.

Both sides used gas in the First World War. At first, it worked: men ran away in panic. Later, however, soldiers learned how to cope with gas attacks. Gas was a terrifying and nasty weapon, but it did not win the war.

TYPES OF GAS

The first kind of gas the Germans used was chlorine – a green cloud which stripped the lining from men's lungs. Later in 1915, the Germans used phosgene, which was even more deadly – it couldn't be seen, and its effects came on slowly, so men breathed it for a while before they realised what was happening. Death by phosgene was horrible and painful, and could take two days as the lungs filled up with yellow pus and the victim died by drowning.

At first, soldiers tried to stop the effects of the gas by holding cloth soaked in urine over their mouths, or by lighting fires to force the gas clouds upwards, but these methods did not work. Later, however, gas masks were invented which stopped the effects of chlorine and phosgene.

In 1917, therefore, the Germans started to use another gas, mustard gas. This was not as deadly – only two out of every 100 victims died. But it burned the soldiers' skin, faces and eyes terribly. After July 1917, mustard gas accounted for 14% of all battlefield casualties.

A SOURCE

60 years later, Jack Dorgan, who was a soldier in 1915, remembers the first gas attack.

We had only gone 100 yards when the gas got us. We had never heard of it before. Our eyes were streaming and hurting, and all we had were our field bandages. So we bandaged each other's eyes, and anyone who could still see led a line of about six men, each holding onto the shoulder of the one in front.

B SOURCE

A soldier, Henry Tonks, describes how the artist John Sargent painted gassed men in July 1918.

Gassed men kept coming in, led in groups of about six, just as Sargent had painted them. They sat on the grass. They were in a lot of pain from their eyes, which were covered in bandages.

The gas was mustard gas, and it makes the men blind for a time. Sargent walked among them making notes.

C SOURCE

British soldiers gassed, 1915–18.

Year	Gassed	Died
1915	12,792	307
1916	6698	1123
1917	52,452	1796
1918	113,764	2673

Gassed men, painted by John Sargent in July 1918.
Compare this painting to Source E.

Gassed British soldiers, April 1918.

The Battle of Loos, September 1915, described by the historian Trevor Wilson in 1986.

There was no wind, but they still used the gas. So it did not work. Some of it did reach the German line and take them by surprise. But most of it hung about in No Man's Land or moved so slowly that the British soldiers ran into it when they attacked.

In some places, it actually blew back onto the British lines and gassed British soldiers.

Controversy!

'It is a thing of shame that the British used poison gas against the Germans in World War One, and our government ought publicly to apologise for doing so.'

What is your INSTANT REACTION?

Questions

a What can you learn from Source A about the first use of gas in April 1915?

b Does Source D support the evidence of Sources A and B about the effects of gas?

c How useful are Sources C and E as evidence about the impact of gas?

d 'Gas was a terrifying but, in the end, unsuccessful weapon.' Using the sources and your own knowledge, explain whether you agree with this view.

Key Issue

- What were aircraft used for during the war?

Key Words
- 'were planes useless'? • reconnaissance
- 'spotting' • 'dog-fights' • 'aces'
- Red Baron • Fokker • RFC • bombs
- River Somme • parachutes • life expectancy

The airplane was only invented in 1903. In 1914 the fastest planes could only fly at 72 mph and one French general said that they would be 'useless' for war.

How wrong he was!   By the end of the war, the French had built 68,000 planes (and lost 52,000 of them in battle).

RECONNAISSANCE

At first, planes were used to spy on enemy lines and movements.   They took photos which could be studied to see if the enemy was getting ready to attack.

'SPOTTING'

Planes were also used to tell the artillery gunners whether they were hitting their target or not.   However, this took a long time because the only way the plane could get the information to the gunners was to fly back and drop a message out of the plane.

NEW TECHNOLOGY

It was not long before pilots took up guns and started to attack enemy planes in the air. They would have 'dog-fights', trying to shoot down their opponents.   '**Aces**' (fighter pilots who shot down a number of enemy planes) became heroes – the most famous was the German known as the 'Red Baron'.

In 1915, German Fokker planes were given a machine gun which fired through the propeller.   For the next year – until British

technology caught up – the British Royal Flying Corps (RFC) lost many planes.

GROUND ATTACK

After 1916, planes also started to carry bombs – one British bomber plane could carry sixteen 50 kg bombs, or one 750 kg bomb.   They were used to bomb ships, factories, railways and docks.

But enemy fighter planes and anti-aircraft guns made this a very dangerous job.   In 1918, when the British tried to bomb German bridges over the River Somme, they lost 150 planes without destroying a single bridge.

CASUALTIES

During the war, 50,000 airmen were killed. Many British pilots died because the RFC would not give them parachutes.   Planes were expensive, and the RFC wanted the pilots to do everything they could to save the plane before they baled out.

The average life expectancy of a pilot on the Western Front was two weeks.

Controversy!

'Of all the consequences of World War One, it is the invention of the airplane as a weapon of war which has had the greatest effect on history.'

What is your INSTANT REACTION?

A French plane shooting down a German plane.

Questions

a What were the three major roles of aircraft in the war?

b Which of these three roles do you think was most important and why?

c Why do you think the ability of the Fokker to fire through its propeller was such an advantage?

d Pilots didn't live very long. Why, then, were so many men keen to volunteer to serve as pilots?

How effective were gas and aircraft as new weapons?

- Read pages 32–33 and list the TWO main strengths and TWO main weaknesses of gas as a weapon of war.
- Read pages 34–35 and list the TWO main strengths and TWO main weaknesses of planes as a means of war.

Which was the more useful invention?

14 NEW WEAPONS: THE TANK

Key Issue

→

How effective was the tank?

Key Words
- Trench Crossing Machine • Water Tanks
  - 10 mm armour • cannons • crew
- steel face-masks • slow • toppled over
  - Somme • Swinton • Haig • 'the Devil'

When it was invented, the tank was at first called a 'Trench Crossing Machine'. However, to keep them secret, the army took them to France in wooden boxes labelled 'Water Tanks', and the name 'tank' stuck.

Tanks had a top speed of about 4 mph. They carried machine guns or small cannon. They had 10 mm-thick steel armour to protect them from bullets. They rolled forward through the enemy trenches, and the soldiers could shelter behind them. Some tanks had bundles of wood (called 'fascines') to drop into trenches so they could get over them. Others carried hooks to pull and break the barbed wire.

Tanks had a crew of eight men. They had a hard job. Inside it was hot and stuffy. When a bullet hit the tank, small splinters of metal broke off and wounded the crew – who had to wear steel face-masks to protect themselves.

The tanks often broke down, got stuck in the mud or toppled over into shell holes. They also moved so slowly that artillery guns could hit them with shells.

A SOURCE

A British tank stuck in a trench after the Battle of Cambrai, 1917.

TANKS ON THE SOMME

B SOURCE

A German newspaperman describes a tank attack in 1916.

When the German troops looked out at dawn, their blood ran cold. Strange metal monsters were crawling towards them across the mud. Nothing could stop them. They spat bullets at our soldiers. 'The Devil is coming,' said the men.

And behind the strange monsters came waves of British soldiers.

C SOURCE

A painting of the tank attack at Cambrai, 1917.

The first time tanks were used was during the Battle of the Somme in September 1916. The man in charge of the tanks, Colonel Swinton, wanted to use lots of them in a huge surprise attack and win a big break-through. General Haig disagreed. The battle was going badly, and he wanted some good news for the newspapers. Haig sent 49 tanks into battle. Only 18 got as far as the German lines. But they were a huge success – the German soldiers ran away in panic.

The tanks often broke down – in August 1918, the British used 430 tanks in the attack on the German lines. After six days, only six were still working.

Nevertheless, some historians believe that the tank played a big part in winning the war – they played a part in the break-through in August 1918 which finally defeated the Germans, and they made the Germans think that they were going to lose the war.

D SOURCE

In 1933, a British soldier remembered an attack on a German **pill box** (a concrete strong point) in 1917.

The tank stuck fast in the mud, but it still managed to blast through the door and kill the 60 Germans inside. Only 29 British soldiers died in the attack, instead of thousands. The tank had shown its qualities.

Controversy!

'The tank in World War One was a joke.'
What is your INSTANT REACTION?

Questions

a What can you learn from Source B about the effectiveness of tanks as a weapon?
b Use Source A and your own knowledge to explain the limitations of tanks as a weapon.
c How useful is Source C as evidence of the way tanks were used during the war? Use Source C and your own knowledge to answer this question.
d 'The tank had shown its qualities.' Is this an accurate interpretation of the role of tanks during the war? Use Source D and your own knowledge to answer this question.

15 THE WAR AT SEA

Key Issue

Why was the war at sea important in winning the war?

Key Words

food • U-boats • *Lusitania* • torpedoes • merchant ships • Q-ships • depth charges • convoys • Zimmerman telegram • America • blockade • Jutland • Jellicoe • Scheer • 'something wrong with our bloody ships' • Hunger Riots

There was only one big sea-battle during the First World War. But some historians believe that the war was won and lost at sea, because neither Britain nor Germany could grow enough to feed their people and needed ships to bring in food. This meant that the side that ruled the sea would win the war.

THE U-BOAT CAMPAIGN AGAINST BRITAIN

The Germans used a new invention – the **U-boat** ('undersea boat') – to sink ships bringing food to Britain.

At first, the Germans only sank British ships. But food came to Britain in ships from many countries. In February 1915, therefore, the Germans said they would sink any ship sailing to Britain.

Up to February 1915, the Germans had only sunk ten British ships. In August 1915 alone they sank 42 ships. Britain came close to losing the war because of the U-boats. At one point, in 1917, Britain had only two month's supply of flour left.

THE SINKING OF THE LUSITANIA

In May 1915, a German U-boat commander attacked a passenger ship, the *Lusitania*. The *Lusitania* was sailing from America to Britain. It exploded and sank in 20 minutes. 1200 men, women and children died.

Unknown to the U-boat captain – as well as its passengers – the *Lusitania* was secretly carrying

bullets and shells to Britain. That is why the ship blew up and sank so quickly (and killed so many people) when he fired on it.

But the sinking of the *Lusitania* was a disaster for the Germans. The British government put out **propaganda** saying that the Germans were cruel killers of civilians. More importantly, 128 Americans were among the dead – the sinking of the *Lusitania* angered Americans and was one of the reasons why America came into the war in 1917.

What do you think – was the U-boat captain right to sink the *Lusitania*?

ANTI-SUBMARINE MEASURES

The British tried different ways to stop the U-boats.

U-boats did not carry many **torpedoes**, so, when they found a ship on its own, U-boat captains came to the surface and sank it with their deck guns. To stop this, the British government started to put guns on **merchant ships**. They also invented the Q-ship – which looked like a merchant ship, but was really a well-armed warship. When the U-boat surfaced to attack what it thought was a merchant ship, the Q-ship would attack it.

The British also invented depth charges (bombs which went off under the water) to attack the U-boats. But because hydrophones (headphones to listen for the sound of U-boats) had not been fully developed by the end of the war, British battleships found it hard to find any U-boats to attack.

In fact, by the end of 1916, the British had only sunk 15 U-boats. Yet by the end of 1916, German U-boats were sinking one in four merchant ships sailing to Britain. Britain was in real danger of losing the war.

What saved Britain in 1916 was the German government! The Germans were frightened of making the Americans angry. In 1916, therefore, they stopped sinking *every* ship sailing to Britain, and went back to sinking only British ships. So Britain was saved – just!

What do you think – should the German government have kept on sinking every ship taking food to Britain?

THE CONVOY SYSTEM

Also, after April 1917, the British started to use **convoys**. Instead of sailing to Britain on their own, merchant ships went over in groups of 20 or more ships, protected by battleships with depth charges.

This made it much harder for the U-boats to attack, even using torpedoes. As soon as they attacked one ship, the battleships knew where they were and could fight back with depth charges. By 1918, the U-boats were only sinking one in 25 merchant ships sailing to Britain.

In February 1917, the Germans took the risk, again, of sinking ALL ships sailing to Britain – even the ships of countries not in the war. Even American ships.

They hoped that Britain would begin to starve, and that the Americans would not get so angry that they would join the war.

THE END OF AMERICAN NEUTRALITY

However, the Germans got it wrong. The Americans did not want to fight Germany, but when Germany began sinking American ships, they declared war on Germany on 6 April 1917.

Another reason America declared war on Germany was the 'Zimmerman telegram'.

In March 1917, Germany tried to make a treaty with Mexico and sent a telegram – in code – offering to give Texas to Mexico if the Mexicans would attack America. The British secret service decoded the telegram and gave it to the American President, who gave it to the American newspapers. It was Germany's sinking of American ships which made the American government declare war, but it was the Zimmerman telegram that got the American people angry enough to support their government.

After 1917, American battleships helped the British battleships protect the convoys. In August 1917, German U-boats sank 211 merchant ships. By August 1918 shipping losses had been halved, and fell rapidly thereafter.

Also, America started sending American wheat to Britain (before, the only wheat going to Britain was from Australia, on the other side of the world). America also lent money to the British government, and sent millions of soldiers to fight on the Western Front.

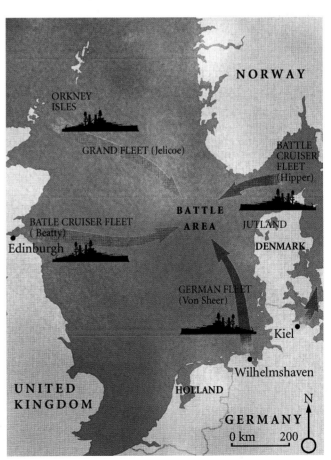

Map of the Battle of Jutland.

THE BATTLE OF JUTLAND, MAY 1916

While the German U-boats were trying to sink British merchant shipping and starve Britain to death, the British navy was blockading German ports to try to starve the Germans to death.

In 1916, the German navy came out to try to break the **blockade**. The British fleet was commanded by Admiral Jellicoe and the Germany fleet by Admiral Scheer. On 31 May 1916 they opened fire on each other. The two fleets were 15 km apart.

The German gunners were much better than the British gunners. Also, the German shells went easily through the British ships and blew up their ammunition stores. Three British ships just blew up. One of the British commanders said: 'There seems to be something wrong with our bloody ships today.'

British losses were much greater. The British lost 14 ships – three of them big battleships – and 6000 men were killed. The Germans lost 11 smaller ships (only one big battleship) and just 2550 men.

WHO WON?

When is a defeat not a defeat?

Although he was winning the battle, Admiral Scheer was worried. The British fleet was much bigger than the German fleet. Scheer knew that if he lost this battle, Germany would lose the war. After a brief battle, he turned away and went back to port. The Germans claimed victory, but they never left port again.

Jellicoe also knew that if *he* lost this battle, Britain would lose the war. He did not try to stop Scheer getting away.

So, although the Germans gave the British navy a bloody nose, the blockade continued. The German people got more and more hungry. Three-quarters of a million Germans died from hunger and disease.

In 1918, they were living on berries and potatoes, there were Hunger Riots in Germany, and the German government was forced to end the war. In this way, Jellicoe's 'defeat' at Jutland won the war!

Controversy!

'Britannia ruled the waves in World War One only because the Germans admirals were such cowards.'

What is your INSTANT REACTION?

HOW THE GUNS ON GERMAN SHIPS WERE BETTER THAN THE BRITISH GUNS

Double closed doors on German gun turrets stopped the explosion from a direct hit travelling down and igniting the ship's magazine. Single open doors on British ships allowed a direct hit to explode the ship's main magazine.

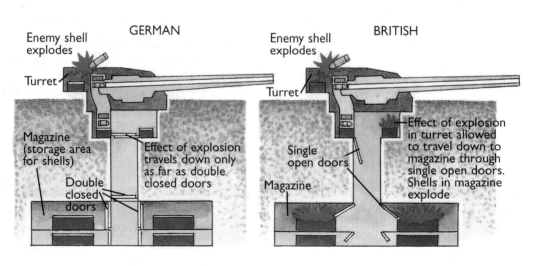

GERMAN

Enemy shell explodes

Turret

Magazine (storage area for shells)

Effect of explosion travels down only as far as double closed doors

Double closed doors

BRITISH

Enemy shell explodes

Turret

Single open doors

Magazine

Effect of explosion in turret allowed to travel down to magazine through single open doors. Shells in magazine explode

A SOURCE

In 1914, the German navy shelled Scarborough, Hartlepool and Whitby.

MEN OF BRITAIN!
WILL YOU STAND THIS?

Nº 2 Wykeham Street, SCARBOROUGH, after the German bombardment on Decr 16th. It was the Home of a Working Man. Four People were killed in this House including the Wife, aged 58, and Two Children, the youngest aged 5.

78 Women & Children were killed and 228 Women & Children were wounded by the German Raiders

ENLIST NOW

B SOURCE

A German sailor remembers the Battle of Jutland.

It was the biggest sea battle ever fought.

We beat the British fleet. Many British battleships were sunk.

D SOURCE

A comment by the British historian Malcolm Brown in 2002.

The British won the Battle of Jutland. The German navy did nothing else until November 1918, when it surrendered.

Questions

a Why was Source A produced by the British government?

b Use Source B and your own knowledge to explain why this sailor believed Jutland was a German victory.

c How useful is Source C as evidence about the Battle of Jutland?

d Is Source D a fair interpretation of the Battle of Jutland? Use Source D and your own knowledge to answer this question.

C SOURCE

A painting by a British artist of the sinking of the British battleship *Invincible*.

Explain each of the following ideas:
- 'The side that ruled the sea would win the war.'
- 'Germany tried to starve Britain to death using U-boats but failed.'
- 'Britain tried to starve Germany to death using a blockade and succeeded.'

Key Issue

Why did the German Spring Offensive fail?

Key Words
- Ludendorff • Spring Offensive • 'Operation Michael' • 'infiltration tactics' • Foch • 8 August 1918 • blockade • naval mutiny • Communists • Germany's allies • armistice

By 1918, some people were saying that the war would go on forever – there seemed to be no end in sight. But, in November 1918, Germany gave up. There were three reasons for this:

1. The last big German attack failed.
2. Two million American soldiers came to France.
3. The German people were starving.

LUDENDORFF'S SPRING OFFENSIVE

In 1918, General Ludendorff, the German commander on the Western Front, made one last try to win the war before the Americans came. Because the Germans had defeated Russia, they also had three-quarters of a million men from the Eastern Front.

The Germans used a new tactic they called 'infiltration tactics'. Instead of attacking along a whole stretch of enemy line, they attacked at a weak point, and drove deep into enemy land. They simply went round enemy strong-points. Then they attacked the enemy artillery and put it out of action so the rest of the German army could follow.

The Germans attacked on 21 March 1918. They called it 'Operation Michael'. They advanced as far in one day as the British had during the whole of the Battle of the Somme. By June, they were only 80 km from Paris. The British and French troops could not retreat fast enough to dig new trenches. It looked as though Germany would win the war.

But the best German soldiers were killed making the break-through. Most important of all, their artillery and supplies could not keep up with the attacks. By the end of July, the German soldiers were tired.

THE ALLIED COUNTER-OFFENSIVE: 8 AUGUST 1918

The German successes had forced the Allied generals also to have a re-think. They put the French Marshal Foch in charge of all their forces. Foch made them all work together to a single plan.

On 8 August 1918, the Allies struck back. Faced by fresh American troops and 600 tanks, the tired German soldiers gave up. Many surrendered. Most of them realised that they could never win the war.

THE GERMAN HOME FRONT

In Germany, too, there was trouble. The British **blockade** was causing food shortages. To try and break the blockade, in October 1918, the government ordered the German navy to go and fight the British navy. The navy refused; the sailors **mutinied**.

The German people were starving and there were food riots. There were strikes for better pay. Some Germans became **Communists** – which worried rich Germans, who did not want a Communist revolution like there had been in Russia.

Germany's allies were just as tired. Turkey dropped out of the war in October, Austria in November. Most Germans realised that they could never win the war.

On 9 November Kaiser Wilhelm gave up the throne of Germany, and the new government agreed to an **armistice** at 11 am on 11 November 1918.

A SOURCE

Years after the war, a German officer, Herbert Sulzbach, remembers a visit home in October 1918.

We hadn't realised at the Front how bad things were at home. There was no food, and the mood of the people was really bad. They were really fed up with the war, and wanted it to end – win or lose. Nobody saluted me. Some of my friends were getting letters which upset them, saying: 'We have nothing to eat. Come back home as soon as you can'.

B SOURCE

German women queuing for potato peelings in 1917.

C SOURCE

Industrial output of the great powers, 1914 (in millions of tons).

Allied Powers	Coal	Iron	Steel
Britain	292	11	6.5
France	40	5	0.5
United States	455	30	32
Central Powers			
Germany	277	15	14
Austria–Hungary	47	2	3

D SOURCE

German deaths as a result of lack of food.

1915	88,000
1916	120,000
1917	260,000
1918	294,000

E SOURCE

A German sailor, Richard Stumpf, writing in his Diary at the end of 1915.

The officers do nothing. We have had our food cut by half – they still have feasts in the officers' room.

*We hope that the ship will hit a **mine** so that the officers' room will be blown to bits.*

F SOURCE

German prisoners near the end of the war.

Questions

a What can you learn from Source A about the Home Front in Germany in 1918?

b Does Source D support the evidence of Sources A and B about how the war affected Germany's civilian population?

c How useful are Sources C and E as evidence of why Germany was defeated in 1918?

d 'Germany was defeated in 1918 because of the failure of Ludendorff's Spring Offensive.' Use the sources, and your own knowledge, to explain whether you agree with this view.

17 THE TREATY OF VERSAILLES

→ **Key Issue**

Was the treaty too harsh?

Key Words

- Kaiser • armistice • 'stab in the back'
- Lloyd George • Clemenceau • Woodrow Wilson • Treaty of Versailles: blame, reparations, land, army • *Deutsch Zeitung*

A 'STAB IN THE BACK'?

Although the final German attack in 1918 was defeated (see pages 42–43), the German army did not collapse. It retreated slowly, without panicking.

When the Kaiser left the throne and the new government made the **armistice**, many German soldiers did not *feel* like they had been defeated. Some soldiers wanted to go on fighting and blamed the new government for betraying the soldiers – they said the government had 'stabbed the army in the back'.

They called the new government 'the November criminals'.

One of the soldiers who believed this was Adolf Hitler, and these ideas helped him come to power in Germany in 1933.

TERMS OF THE TREATY

If some Germans were angry about the armistice, they were even more angry about the Treaty of Versailles.

Lloyd George (the British Prime Minister, 1916–22) and Georges Clemenceau (the French Prime Minister) openly said they wanted to 'make Germany pay' – although the American President, Woodrow Wilson, tried to get a fairer peace.

The Treaty of Versailles, which Germany was forced to sign in June 1919, said:

1. Germany had to accept the blame for starting the war.
2. Germany had to pay £6.6 billion (called 'reparations') to repair the damage 'Germany' had done in the war.
3. Germany had to hand over land to France and Poland, and had to give all its colonies to Britain and France.
4. Germany's armed forces were cut – Germany was allowed an army of only 100,000 men, and no planes, U-boats or tanks at all.

Germans blamed their new government for accepting these harsh terms, and this was another thing that helped Hitler come to power.

A SOURCE

On 7 November 1918, four days before the war ended, a British army chaplain wrote this about the **morale** of the German army.

The Germans are defending well, and killing many of our men. We all – except our generals, who do not know how determined the German soldiers are – expect another six months fighting.

B SOURCE

German soldiers returning to Berlin are greeted like heroes.

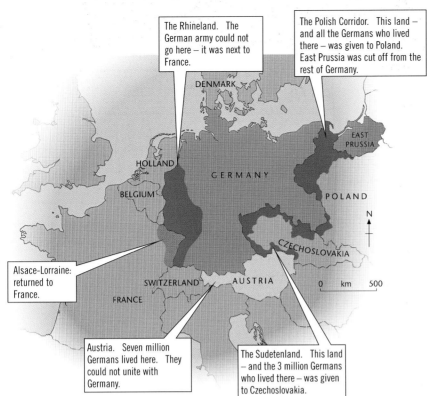

The Rhineland. The German army could not go here – it was next to France.

The Polish Corridor. This land – and all the Germans who lived there – was given to Poland. East Prussia was cut off from the rest of Germany.

Alsace-Lorraine: returned to France.

Austria. Seven million Germans lived here. They could not unite with Germany.

The Sudetenland. This land – and the 3 million Germans who lived there – was given to Czechoslovakia.

DENMARK
HOLLAND
BELGIUM
GERMANY
EAST PRUSSIA
POLAND
CZECHOSLOVAKIA
SWITZERLAND
AUSTRIA
FRANCE
N
0   km   500

Map of the Treaty of Versailles.

C SOURCE

In October 1918 General Ludendorff said this about the German army.

I tell you this.   8 August 1918 was a black day in the history of the German army. Many soldiers refused to fight.

The morale of the men was bad, because they had no potatoes.

The new soldiers were second rate, and would not obey orders.

D SOURCE

Adolf Hitler wrote this in 1924.

The miserable gang of politicians betrayed the German people to line their own pockets.

I said they should be hanged, because they let Germany lose the war.

F SOURCE

This was printed in the German newspaper, *Deutsch Zeitung*, on 20 June 1919.

Revenge!   Germans!   Today the shameful Treaty is being signed.   Do not forget it. We must work to re-conquer our place as leader of the world.   Then we will get revenge for the shame of 1919.

E SOURCE

In the last months of 1918 there were **Communist** rebellions in Germany.

Questions

a What can you learn from Source A about the state of the German army in the later stages of the war?

b Does Source C support the evidence of Sources A and B about the morale of the German army in 1918?

c How useful are Sources D and E as evidence of conditions in Germany at the end of the war?

d 'Germany lost the war because its army was "stabbed in the back" by the politicians at home.'   Use the sources, and your own knowledge, to explain whether you agree with this view.

<u>18</u> WOMEN AND THE HOME FRONT

→ **Key Issue**

How far did the war really change the lives of women in Britain?

Key Words
- Votes for Women • Oxford University
- doctors and lawyers • Lady Astor
- Marie Stopes • 'right to serve' • munitions
- 'canaries' • shipyards • trams • ambulances
- Women's Land Army • post-war 'clear-out'

The **feminist** writer Germaine Greer said that women in the First World War were like a bird whose cage is left open – they had a look outside, but decided life was better back in the cage. By this, she meant that women had a taste of freedom and equality during the war, but gave it away again when the war was over.

BEFORE 1914

Few upper-class women worked.

Some single middle-class women worked as teachers, nurses, typists, and as sales assistants in posh department stores. But most gave up work when they married. In some jobs, like teaching, they had to give up work when they married.

Working-class women worked, usually in factories or as maids in rich houses – many of them even after they were married. A maid might earn as little as £2 a month.

CHANGES AFTER THE WAR

One huge thing that changed for all women after the war was that, in 1918, women over 30 were allowed to vote.

The war changed some things for middle-class women. In 1919:
- Oxford University allowed women to study for degrees for the first time.
- Women were allowed for the first time to work as doctors and lawyers.
- Women were allowed to stand for Parliament (and Lady Astor was elected as the first women MP).

It is important not to exaggerate these changes. Men could vote at age 21 – a right not given to women until 1928. And few women went into the top jobs – in 1911 women made up 6% of people in the top jobs; in 1951, women still only counted for 8%.

Working-class women also gained from the war. In 1921:
- Marie Stopes opened the first birth control clinic – for married women only. For the first time, women began to wonder whether their life had to be nothing but having and looking after children.

'THE RIGHT TO SERVE'

At first, the government would not allow women to help with the war.

Before the war, the **Suffragettes** had demanded the right to vote. Now, in 1915, 60,000 Suffragettes went on a march to demand 'the right to serve'. The government was forced to give way – especially because *someone* had to do the jobs of the millions of men who had gone to fight in the war.

Some of the jobs done by women were:
- Making shells in **munitions** factories – very dangerous work, especially because the chemicals gave them cancer (they were nick-named 'the canaries' because the girls' skin turned yellow). But the girls earned up to £5 a week; a very good wage for a woman.
- Shipyard workers;
- Tram drivers;
- Ambulance drivers; and
- Farm workers ('the Women's Land Army').

HOW MUCH REALLY CHANGED DURING THE WAR?

It is true that 700,000 women went to work in industry, and that this was vital for the war effort.

However, it is important not to exaggerate the scale of the changes.

- Only a third of the new workers who went into industry were women.
- Most of the women who went to work in industry already worked before the war.
- Even before the war, most of the shells were made by women workers.
- Most of the women who went to work in industry did not do skilled jobs and were not taught how to do them.
- Many women in industry were given a hard time by the men workers, who did not want them.

THE POST-WAR 'CLEAR OUT'

After the war, half the women who had gone to work left their jobs and let the men returning from the war have them. 1920–21 was a bad time for industry, and most of the other half were sacked.

In 1911, women had made up 32% of the working population – in 1921 they made up only 31%.

It seems that, as far as jobs go, women had by 1921 lost everything that had been gained during the war.

> ### Controversy!
> 'It is just wishful thinking to say that the first World War improved the place of women in our society. Women actually allowed themselves to be exploited during the war – to be used, and then discarded. Far from advancing the women's cause, the First World War set it back. And the worst thing is that it was their own fault.'
> **What is your INSTANT REACTION?**

A NEW GENERATION

But one thing had changed. Women now *knew* that they could be every bit as good as a man. This did not change things immediately, but it had great effects as time went on.

One thing that did change, therefore, was the way some women behaved. The 1920s were the time of the '**flappers**' – young women who went out on their own to the pub, smoked in public, wore the latest fashions and danced the latest dances.

So, looking over pages 46–49, do you agree with Germaine Greer – did women 'open the cage', look out, and decide that life was better inside the cage?

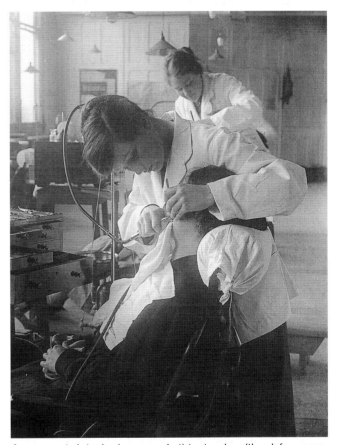

A government photo showing women dentists at work – although few women managed to keep such exciting, well-paid jobs after the war.

A 1920s 'flapper', with short skirt and cigarette. Why do you think she had her hair cut short like a man's?

A SOURCE

A poster showing women workers making shells — 'for king and country'.

Controversy!

'The so-called "women's contribution to the war" that feminist historians talk about was just window-dressing. It was the men who did the fighting, the suffering – the dying.'

What is you INSTANT REACTION

B SOURCE

A British women, Daisy Collingwood, remembering, 80 years later, her war work making shells.

I loved the job. Before the war I'd lived in the country but now to work with lots of people was just heaven. I was important. I did the night shift and stayed up all night for the first time in my life.

Mum and dad tried to get me to give it up, but I didn't. For the first time I was living my own life.

C SOURCE

The title of this government photo for the Women's Land Army was: 'Sunshine in the Cowshed'.

D SOURCE

A comment made by the historian Trevor Wilson in 1996.

Before the war, people had said that, if someone had to go without work, it ought to be the woman. The war did not change anything.

Questions

a What can you learn from Source A about the role of women in the First World War?

b Use Source B and your own knowledge to explain why women were so keen to work in munitions factories?

c How useful is Source C as evidence about the work women did in the Women's Land Army?

d Is Source D a fair interpretation of how the war affected the position of women as workers? Use Source D and your own knowledge to answer this question.

Under the title 'How did the war affect the position of women in society?', write two sentences to say what life was like for women before the war, then list:
- five things women did during the war;
- five things that changed for women because of the war; and
- seven things that did not change much.

Controversy!

'Change comes from doing, not talking. The women munitions workers of World War One had ten times the impact of the Suffragettes on men's attitudes to women. By contrast, the Suffragettes seem silly and over-emotional.'

What is your INSTANT REACTION?

Key Issue

- What role did women play in Britain's armed forces?

THE ROSES OF NO MAN'S LAND

When war broke out, many women became nurses, and some of them went to the Western Front, although only women at least 23 years old were allowed to do so.

Also, 80,000 women **volunteered** to join the Voluntary Aid Detachments (VADs). VAD nurses were given basic First Aid training, and 8000 of them went to the Western Front. Most VAD nurses were rich women, because they were not paid.

The nurses were called 'The Roses of No Man's Land' after a song of the time. But working with the wounded and dying was an upsetting and nasty job. One women remembered: 'The leg I was holding came off with a jerk, and I dropped it in the bucket with all the other arms and legs.'

EDITH CAVELL

The work was not just upsetting and nasty. Nurses who worked close to the Front Line were in danger from shells.

Edith Cavell was a British nurse who ended up working behind German lines in Belgium. She helped British soldiers escape back to France. The Germans shot her as a spy in 1915 – although it made the German government very unpopular in Britain and America.

THE WOMEN'S SERVICES

At first, the government would not let women join the armed forces. As the war went on, and more and more men were needed to fight, in 1917 it changed its mind. Women served in:

- The Women's Army Auxiliary Corps (WAAC);
- The Women's Royal Naval Service (WRNS); and
- The Women's Royal Air Force (WRAF).

Women were allowed to be secretaries and cooks, and this let the army send the men to fight.

WAACs soon got a bad name for being too friendly with the men, and people were outraged when 21 of them (out of 6000) got pregnant.

THE WOMEN'S LAND ARMY

A quarter of a million farm workers went to fight in the war, so the government set up the Women's Land Army to try to get women to fill their jobs. With the **U-boat** attacks, it was important that Britain grew as much food as possible.

48,000 women joined the Women's Land Army, but this was not enough, and the government had to bring men back from the front. Most people did not see farm work – which was dirty and heavy work – as a 'woman's job'.

Controversy!

'We put up statues to great male war leaders like Winston Churchill and the Duke of Wellington. Everything about this is wrong. We should put up statues to Edith Cavell – SHE, not they, represents everything that we should admire.'

What is your INSTANT REACTION?

A SOURCE

Alice Proctor, who was 19 when she went to France as a VAD nurse, remembered this about her training.

I was told how to stop bleeding, and how to use broomsticks to set a broken leg, and how to give sweet tea for shock (which of course is wrong). For burns, amazingly, we were told to put on flour (which of course is wrong). You just picked up things as you went along.

B SOURCE

A poster of 1917 asking women to join the Women's Land Army.

NATIONAL SERVICE
WOMEN'S LAND ARMY

"GOD SPEED THE PLOUGH
AND THE WOMAN WHO DRIVES IT"

APPLY FOR ENROLMENT FORMS AT YOUR NEAREST POST OFFICE OR
EMPLOYMENT EXCHANGE

C SOURCE

A British poster from 1915.

WOMEN OF BRITAIN SAY — "GO!"

D SOURCE

A comment on women in the First World War made by a modern historian in 1986.

The part played by women was of no real use to the war effort. But it stopped the soldiers worrying what would happen to their families if they were killed.

Questions

a What can you learn from Source A about the training given to women in the VADs?

b Why was Source B distributed in Britain in 1917? Use Source B and your own knowledge to answer this question.

c How useful is Source C to an historian studying the role of women in the First World War? Use Source C and your own knowledge to answer this question.

d Is Source D a fair interpretation of the role played by women in the First World War? Use Source D and your own knowledge to answer this question.

20 CIVILIAN HARDSHIP

Key Words

- U-boats • food • gardens • potato • fixed price of bread • rationing • punishments • Scarborough, Hartlepool and Whitby • Zeppelins • bombers • shops with German-sounding names • Windsor family

RATIONING

The German **U-boat** attacks made the government worry that Britain would run out of food, but it did not want to bring in **rationing** because it would look like the Germans were winning. So at first the government did other things.

1. It tried to get people to grow their own food in their gardens, and keep chickens.
2. It tried to get people to use less food – for example, it asked people to go without meat one day a week.
3. It allowed bakers to add things to the bread, so that they would use less flour. Most bakers added potato – people complained about the taste, but bread was never rationed.
4. When the price of bread went up, the government fixed the price at a level people could afford.

DO NOT FEED THE DOG

Eventually, however, the government did bring in some rationing of things that were in short supply – things like sugar, meat and butter. Some people said that this was interfering too much in people's lives, although there was never large-scale rationing like in the Second World War.

But there were harsh punishments for people who broke the rules. One woman was fined £20 for feeding steak to her dog, and a man was fined £50 for giving bread to his pigs. And the punishment for stealing a ration book was three months in prison.

ENEMY ACTION

For the first time in a war, the enemy made attacks on the British people at home.

1. In 1914, the German navy shelled Scarborough, Hartlepool and Whitby, killing and wounding 700 people.
2. After 1915, there were **Zeppelin** raids over London, which killed about 150 people.
3. After 1917, German bomber planes attacked British towns. One raid on London killed 162 people, including 16 children hiding in the cellar of a school.

German attacks killed about 2000 people – many fewer than the 66,000 British civilians who died in the Second World War. But it frightened people, and it made them hate the Germans – in 1915 people attacked shops owned by people with German-sounding names.

One side-effect was that the royal family changed their name from their proper German name (Saxe-Coburg-Gotha) to Windsor, to make it sound more 'English'!

A SOURCE

Sybil Morrison described in 1916 what happened when a Zeppelin was shot down.

The bag part was on fire, and we knew that there were 60 people in it, burning to death.

I was upset to see kind, good British people dancing in the streets as they watched 60 people being burned alive.

B SOURCE

A poster published by the British government in 1917.

We risk our lives to bring you food.
It's up to you not to waste it.

'A Message from our Seamen'

D SOURCE

A comment by the historian John Brooman in 1985.

By 1917, many people were not so happy to be at war, because it was changing their lives in ways they did not like.

Questions

a Look at Source A. Why did British civilians react in this way to the shooting down of a Zeppelin?

b Why did the British government issue posters like Source B in 1917? Use Source B and your own knowledge to answer this question.

c How useful is Source C to an historian studying the effect of German air raids on Britain?

d Is Source D an accurate interpretation of civilian attitudes to the war by the end of 1916? Use Source D and your own knowledge to answer this question.

C SOURCE

Results of a Zeppelin air raid.

21 STATE CONTROL

Key Words

- conscription • 'scandal of the shells'
- Ministry of Munitions • nationalisation: railways, shipyards, mines, flour mills
- DORA: pubs, censorship, Bonfire Night
- war bonds

During the war, the government greatly increased its control over industry and people's lives.

The Liberal government that was in power before 1914 did not think that state control of industry or personal freedoms was a good idea. That is why it delayed **conscription** until 1916 – it wanted people to be able to decide for themselves whether they wanted to fight.

THE MUNITIONS SCANDAL

The first thing which made the government realise that greater state control was necessary was 'the scandal of the shells'. In 1915 the army complained that they did not have enough weapons to fight the war. British firms were only making 250 shells a day – the army needed millions. Prices were high and quality was poor.

Asquith (who was Prime Minister 1908–16) set up a 'Ministry of **Munitions**' with Lloyd George in charge. The government built munitions factories and took over many private firms. Shell production increased from half a million in 1914 to almost 90 million in 1917.

STATE CONTROL

The government soon realised that what was right for shells was right for many other things as well. By the end of the war, the government had taken control of all production of weapons, aircraft and farm machinery. It had also **nationalised** the railways, shipyards, coal mines and flour mills.

DORA

The Defence of the Realm Act (DORA) of 1915 also gave the government great control over ordinary people's lives. Bank holidays and Bonfire Night were cancelled. It was made illegal to work at trades such as house-painting (which weren't needed for the war effort) or to talk about army movements. The newspapers were not allowed to print stories which might harm the **morale** of the people. Workers in munitions factories were not allowed to strike.

Before the war, pubs had been able to open at 5 am, and some workers went to work drunk. To stop this, DORA invented the idea of pub 'opening hours'. Beer was watered down to make it less alcoholic, and people were forbidden to buy a 'round' – one man was fined for buying his wife a drink. Arrests for drunkenness fell to a tenth of their pre-war level.

A SOURCE

70 years after the war, a soldier remembered the shortage of shells in 1915.

We ran out of shells. We were allowed only 60 a week.

We did not know whether to annoy the Germans by firing ten a day, or whether to save them all up for one big attack.

LEND YOUR
FIVE SHILLINGS
TO YOUR COUNTRY
AND

CRUSH
THE GERMANS

People were asked to buy 'war bonds' – a way of lending money to the government.

B SOURCE

A *Punch* cartoon of 1915. Lloyd George makes sure the shells get to the soldiers.

DELIVERING THE GOODS.

D SOURCE

A comment made by the historian Niall Ferguson in 1998.

Led by the hero Lloyd George, the British magnificently made the weapons needed.

C SOURCE

A letter to *The Times* newspaper from the owner of a munitions factory, 17 June 1915.

*The problem with making shells is not that the workers are **shirkers**, but that so many men are joining up because people call them cowards if they stay. Good men are leaving my factory, although they could help the war effort much more by making shells.*

Why not give munitions workers a soldier's uniform? This would make them look important, and stop them feeling that they were running away from the war.

Questions

a What does Source A suggest about the supply of artillery shells?
b Why did *Punch* magazine publish Source B in 1915? Use Source B and your own knowledge to answer this question.
c How useful is Source C to an historian studying 'the scandal of the shells' of 1915?
d Is Source D an accurate interpretation of how Britain coped with the demands of the war? Use Source D and your own knowledge to answer this question.

22 A FAIRER, BETTER BRITAIN?

Key Issues

- How did the war affect the power of government?
- How did the war affect living standards?

Key Words

- 'A land fit for heroes': schools, hospitals, council houses • Income Tax • living standards: wages, rents, price of bread, no unemployment, rationing • Treasury Agreement • shop stewards • miners • shipyard workers • Long-term results: Trade Unions, Labour Party, nationalisation of the coal mines

WHAT CHANGED?

In the short term, the war was horrible for both the soldiers and the people at home.

But, in the long term, the war greatly changed a number of things, and improved people's lives.

A 'LAND FIT FOR HEROES'?

When the war was over, Lloyd George said that, now the war against Germany was won, the government ought to try to make Britain 'a land fit for heroes'. Soldiers who had risked their lives for their country deserved good schools for their children, good hospitals if they were sick, and council houses to live in if they could not afford to buy their own. And it is true that, in the next ten years, the government worked hard to provide these things.

At first, however, the government found difficulty in keeping Lloyd George's promises. **Income Tax** had increased during the war from 6% to 30%, and people did not want to keep on paying such high taxes. Also, the government had borrowed £7 billion to pay for the war, and that had to be paid back too.

HOW DID THE WAR AFFECT LIVING STANDARDS?

Wages almost doubled during the war, but prices more than doubled, so some historians think that the standard of living fell. However, there were some things that meant that poor people did quite well out of the war:

1. The government fixed rents through the whole of the war, which was good for people who rented their house – mostly poorer people.
2. The government reduced the price of bread, which was good for poor people.
3. With so many men away as soldiers, there was almost no unemployment at home – and lots of overtime.
4. **Rationing** helped to share food more fairly, which was good for poorer people.

However, the war was not good for some people:

- Teachers' wages did not rise at all, so – with prices rising quickly – they were much worse off.
- Sometimes, where the man had been the family breadwinner but went off to join the army, the family was much worse off.

LLOYD GEORGE AND THE UNIONS

To win the war, Lloyd George needed the factories to produce as much as they could. To do this, he needed the workers on his side.

THE TREASURY AGREEMENT, MARCH 1915

Therefore, in March 1915 Lloyd George met with **Trade Union** leaders to try to come to an agreement. The result was the Treasury Agreement of March 1915.

The unions agreed:

1. To let unskilled workers do the work of skilled men.
2. To ban strikes in 6000 **munitions** factories. Workers could be fined for going on strike or just missing work.
3. Skilled workers were not allowed to change jobs without the government's permission.

The government promised:

1. This agreement would be for the war only – after the war things would go back to what they were.
2. Unskilled workers doing skilled jobs would be paid at the skilled rate – they would not be used as 'cheap labour'.
3. The government would tax highly the profits made by firms supplying the army.
4. The government would keep down the price of bread.

Some workers were not happy with this agreement. They said that the Trade Unions had given away too much. They elected '**shop stewards**' and caused trouble when they thought the workers were being harmed. Lloyd George had to deal with these workers. He did so in two ways:

THE CARROT . . .

When 200,000 South Wales miners went on strike in 1915, Lloyd George just gave in and increased their wages. Coal production had to be kept going.

. . . AND THE STICK

When shipyard workers in Glasgow went on strike, at first Lloyd George met with 3000 shop stewards and tried to get them to stop. When they did not call off the strike, however, he said: 'There is German money up there'. He had the strike leaders arrested, and fined any worker who did not go back to work.

The number of days lost in strikes in Britain during the First World War:

1914	9,900,000
1915	3,000,000
1916	2,400,000
1917	5,600,000
1918	5,900,000

CONSEQUENCES

All in all, the war helped the working classes a lot:

1. The Trade Unions had proved that they cared about the country, as well as the workers. By the end of the war the Trade Unions had eight million members and became very powerful.
2. The Labour Party had proved that it cared about the country, as well as the working classes. After the war, the Liberal Party lost power, and the Labour Party became one of the two main political parties (with the Conservatives). In 1924, Britain got its first Labour government.

America lent $20 billion to help the British war effort. What is the message of this poster?

3. After the war, the government gave back the mines to the mine owners. But the war had proved that the mines were much better run when the government controlled them. Twenty years later (1947), a Labour government **nationalised** the mines, which was much better for the miners.

feed the guns with WAR BONDS and help to end the War

The government wanted people to lend them money by buying war bonds.

South Wales miners.

Looking back over pages 46–59, write an essay 'How much did the First World War change the lives of the people of Britain', using the writing frame below. In each paragraph, remember to talk about *how* what happened *changed people's lives*.
Set out your answer like this:

First sentence
Write that not many civilians were killed in the war, but that the war changed life in three important ways:

Paragraph 1
Write about how the government controlled things like industry and people's lives. Key words and phrases to mention include:
rents, rationing, the price of bread, Treasury Agreement, Ministry of Munitions, strikes, DORA, wages, and Bonfire Night.

Paragraph 2
Write about how women's lives changed. Key words and phrases to mention include:
'the right to serve', 'canaries', VADs, WAAC, WRNS, WRAF, and the Women's Land Army.

Paragraph 3
Write about how the war affected people's lives after the war ended. Key words and phrases to mention include:
'a land fit for heroes', Labour government, Trade Unions, nationalisation, votes for women, birth control, flappers, and pub opening hours.

Conclusion
Finish by explaining how much you think these changes affected people's lives, and for how long.

How to write about sources is as important in the exam as knowing what happened. You must practise this until you can do it.

EDEXCEL

The sources on which these examples are based are on pages 10–13.

(a) *What can you learn from Source A about the Battle of Mons?* [4 marks]

TECHNIQUE
- To get more than two marks for this question you must make an **inference** (i.e. something that the source *suggests* or *implies*).
- Start each idea with the same phrase each time: i.e 'Source A suggests...'.

Example:
Source A suggests that the German generals didn't care about the lives of their men and that sticking to their plan was more important.

It also suggests that the British army was not ready for this battle because it says that they were defeated because they did not have enough men.

(b) *Does Source C support the evidence of Sources A and B about the Battle of Mons?* [6 marks]

TECHNIQUE
- To get high marks, you must talk about *how much* the sources agree.
- Do not compare Source A with B or write about whether the sources are reliable or who wrote them. You will get no marks for this.
- Do not compare Source C with Sources A and B together.

Example:
Source C says that the British were 'in danger of finding themselves alone' and this is supported by A where it says that they were 'in danger of being surrounded'. However, C does not say that the French withdrew or that the British retreated.

There isn't much in C which supports B. Source B talks about how the British were shooting down the Germans and there is nothing in C about this. However, B does say 'In the end there were enough of them to shove us out of the field' and this is supported by the point in C about the British having to retreat.

On balance, C mostly supports A and, to a lesser extent, B.

- Note the use of 'however', and 'On balance' in the final sentence.

(c) *How useful are Sources D and E as evidence of the reasons for the failure of the Schlieffen Plan?* [8 marks]

TECHNIQUE
- You MUST mention the **provenance** and purpose of the sources to get a high mark.
- ALL sources are useful for something, even if they are not reliable.

Example:
Source D could be useful in explaining why the Plan failed because we learn how easily the defenders could kill attackers. However, it doesn't tell us how many machine guns the BEF had; if it was only a few, they wouldn't have made much difference.

Source E is useful, because you might not normally think about the Eastern Front as a reason for the failure of the Schlieffen Plan. Also, it is written by two secondary historians who have been able to take a thoughtful overview of the whole war, so it is likely to be reliable.

(d) *'The Schlieffen Plan failed because of the British role at the Battle of Mons.' Use the sources, and your own knowledge, to explain whether you agree with this view.* [12 marks]

TECHNIQUE
- Don't just say whether you agree or disagree. First give the argument that suggests yes. Then give the argument that supports no.
- Don't go through the sources one after the other. Group them into those which support the point of view of the question and those which do not.
- You don't have to mention all the sources, but make sure you write about most of them.
- Use both the sources and your own knowledge, or you lose half the marks. Flag up your own knowledge by starting the sentence with: 'From my own knowledge...'.
- Finish with a judgement and support it with a short explanation.

Example:
There are some sources which support this view. B suggests the British killed a lot of Germans, C says that the British slowed the Germans down.

However, other sources contradict this opinion. E suggests that the Russians played a more important role. From my own knowledge I know that the German soldiers became very tired, and that the French turned back the Germans at the Marne.

In conclusion, it is probably not true that the Schlieffen Plan failed because of the British at Mons. There were many other reasons the Plan failed, some of which seem more important.

- Do NOT use the words 'I think…'.

AQA

The sources on which these examples are based are on pages 2–3.

(a) *What does Source A tell us about the sort of men who **volunteered** to fight in 1914?* [3 marks]

TECHNIQUE
- This is an easy question, and all you need to do is to provide three ideas – either bits of information from the source, or **inferences**.
- You will get no credit for adding knowledge of your own.
- Do not waste time by writing too much here.

Example 1:
Source A tells us that some of the men who volunteered were criminals. One had been arrested for stealing from German shops. Men arrested for stealing were given the choice of going to prison or joining up.

Example 2:
*Source A suggests that not all the men who joined the army in 1914 were full of **patriotism**. Some joined up to escape going to prison rather than because of a sense of duty.*

(b) *Use Source B and your own knowledge to explain why men volunteered for the army in the early years of the war.* [6 marks]

TECHNIQUE
- Use both the sources and your own knowledge.
- To get a high mark, you must give more than one reason. Also, you must mention the provenance and the purpose of the source.

Example:
*This poster tries to get people to join up because they love their country. The poster also suggests that men who didn't volunteer were '**shirkers**'.*

From my own knowledge I do know that many people joined up because of patriotism. However, this is a government poster which is going to be biased. Also, some men joined up to escape from unemployment or just to impress the girls!

(c) *How useful is Source C as evidence of the British public's reaction to the outbreak of war? Use Source C and your own knowledge to answer this question.* [8 marks]

TECHNIQUE
- You need to make use of the source's provenance and purpose to score top marks.
- You should also test its usefulness by comparing it with your own knowledge.
- Don't confuse usefulness with reliability – an unreliable source can still be useful.

Example:
This photo is useful because it shows lots of people cheering for the war. Although photos can be faked – it is probably a reliable record of what actually happened. From my own knowledge, I know that this is how most people felt about the war, because more than three-quarters of a million men volunteered to join up in the first two months of the war.

*However, this is just a photo of one group of people, who had gone to cheer. Not all people might have felt this way. I know that some people were **Conscientious Objectors**, and it is common sense that some people were scared by the war.*

(d) *Is Source D a fair interpretation of why men volunteered for the army in the First World War? Use Source D and your own knowledge to answer this question.* [8 marks]

TECHNIQUE
- Don't just say whether you agree or disagree. First give the argument that suggests yes. Then give the argument that says no.
- You need to make use of the source's provenance and purpose to get a high mark.
- You should test the source's usefulness by comparing it with your own knowledge.

Example:
The reasons given in the source are those of Robert Burns and not everybody was the same. From my own knowledge, I know that some people joined up to escape unemployment or prison.

However, I know that the excitement which led Burns to join up affected thousands like him who thought that the war would be easy and 'over by Christmas'. Also, his joining up with 'a lot of boys my age' ties in with what we know about the 'Pals' who all joined up together.

In addition, we have no reason to suspect that he might not be telling the truth – he would have no reason to lie to the interviewer more than 80 years after the event.

- Note the use of connectives like 'also', 'in addition' and 'however'.

GLOSSARY

ace – fighter pilot who has shot down a number of enemy planes.

alliances – agreements between countries to support each other if there is a war.

Armistice – the ceasefire signed on 11 November 1918.

artillery – big guns.

attrition – slowly 'wearing down' an opponent.

battalion – division of an army, about 1000 men.

bayonet – the knife attached to the end of a rifle.

Blighty – the soldiers' word for Britain.

blockade – where a navy besieges a country's ports to prevent **merchant ships** coming or going.

censorship – where a government controls the media to stop people learning things it believes would damage **morale**.

Communists – people who believe that the state should own the means of production.

Conscientious Objectors – people who refused to join the army because of their beliefs.

conscription – the government told men aged 18–41 that they HAD to go to join the army.

convoy – a group of merchant ships travelling together for safety.

craters – holes made by shells, **mines** or bombs.

creeping barrage – artillery fire slowly moving forward in front of advancing soldiers.

fatigues – everyday maintenance work done by soldiers, such as repairing the barbed wire.

Feminist – person who believes in rights for women.

Flappers – young women who lived fast and, for the time, had scandalous social lives in the 1920s.

Income Tax – where people pay a proportion of their income in taxes.

inference – something suggested/implied if you 'read between the lines'.

infiltration tactics – the German tactic of 1918 of breaking through along only a small front.

merchant ship – a ship carrying food or goods.

mine – (trench warfare) a tunnel dug under enemy trenches where explosives were detonated; (naval) a floating bomb.

morale – the mood or spirit of the people.

munitions – weapons, especially shells and bullets.

mutiny – where soldiers or sailors rebel against their officers.

nationalised – where the government takes over the running of an industry.

patriotism – love of your country.

pill box – a concrete strong point.

propaganda – where the media is controlled to make people think in a certain way.

provenance – the origin of an historical source (e.g. the author and book), with details of date and context.

rationing – fixing the amounts of food and goods people can buy, to ensure a fair distribution.

reparations – the payments which the Treaty of Versailles said the Germans had to make to 'repair' the damage done during the war.

sap – a short trench leading off from the main trench system.

shirkers – a hate-word for people who weren't doing their bit for the war effort.

Shop Stewards – a **trade unionist** elected by the workers in a factory to represent them.

shrapnel – a splinter of metal which breaks off an exploding bomb.

Socialists – people who believe that the wealth of society should be owned and shared by everyone.

Special Policeman – a volunteer policeman.

stalemate – where neither side can defeat the other.

Suffragettes – women who tried to get the vote in 1903–14 by a campaign of violence.

torpedoes – underwater missiles of a submarine.

Trade Union – an organisation which represents the workers – especially their pay and conditions.

U-boat – a submarine ('undersea boat').

volunteer – someone who offers to join an organisation because they want to.

Zeppelin – German airship.

INDEX

The publishers would like to thank the following individuals, institutions and companies for permission to reproduce copyright illustrations in this book:
Imperial War Museum, London: pp 2, 6, 7, 9, 10, 12 16, 19 (top and bottom), 23 (top and bottom), 28, 29, 33 (bottom), 36, 41 (top), 43 (right), 44, 47, 48 (bottom), 49, 51 (left and right), 53 (bottom); © Michael St. Maur Sheil/CORBIS: p 13; John Singer Sargent *Gassed*, 1918/ ©IWM # 1460: p 33 (top); The Art Archive: p3; Australian War Memorial: p 4; Punch: pp 5, 55 (right); The Art Archive/Australian War Memorial: p 25; AKG Images: pp 31 (left), 45; Mary Evans Picture Library: p 35; The Art Archive/ Imperial War Museum: p 41 (bottom); Ullstein Bild Berlin: p 43 (left); Hulton Archive/Getty Images: pp 48 (top), 59; The Art Archive/ Imperial War Museum/Eileen Tweedy: p 58.

Text Acknowledgements.
All sources have been adapted to make them more accessible to students.
Abacus for the extract from *The Bloody Game* edited by P Fussell (1991); Andromeda Oxford Ltd for extracts from *The Experience of World War I* by J M Winter (1988); Arnold for the extract from *Octobrists to Bolsheviks* by M McCauley (1984); BBC Books for the extracts from *1914-1918* by J Winter and B Baggett (1996); BBC TV for material from *Time Watch* (1996); Collins for material from *People's Century* by G Hodgson (1995); Constable and Robinson Ltd for the extract from *Nurse at the Russian Front* by F Farmborough (1974); Croom Helm Ltd for extracts from *Eye in Deep Hell* by J Ellis (1979); extracts from *Forgotten Voices of the Great War* by Max Arthur published by Ebury, used by permission of The Random House Group Limited; Granada Publishing for the extract from *The War in the Trenches* by A Lloyd (1976); R Hale Ltd for extracts from *The War Walk* by N Jones (1983); Harrap for the extract from *I Saw Them Die* by S Millard (1936); Heinemann Publishers for the concept of 'crossing the T' from *History and Teaching and Historical Understanding* by A K Dickinson and P J Lee; Leo Cooper for extracts from *The Price of Pity* by M Stephen (1996) and *Veterans* by R van Emden and S Humphries (1998); Longman for the extract from *The Great War* by J Brooman (1985); Pan Books for the extracts from *The Firsy World War* by M Brown (2002) and *The Somme* by M Brown (1996); Penguin for extracts from *1914-1918 Voices and Images of the Great War* by L MacDonald (1988), *Death's Men* by D Winter (1979), *Dictionary of Modern History* by D Townson (1998), *The First Day of the Somme* by M Middlebrook (1971) and *The Pity of War* by N Ferguson (1998); Polity Press for the extracts from *The Myriad Faces of War* by T Wilson (1986); Sidgwick and Jackson for extracts from *The Imperial War Museum Book of the First World War* by M Brown (1991); SPA books for the extract from *Tank Warfare* by F Mitchell (1933); the illustration showing 'why soldiers feared going over the top' redrawn, with permission, from an illustration taken from *Key History for Key Stage 3: The Twentieth-Century World* (Stanley Thornes (Publishers) Ltd, 1995); Wellfleet Press for the extract from *The Poster in History* by M Gallo (1989).

The publishers will be glad to make suitable arrangements with any copyright holders whom it has not been possible to contact.

Artwork on pp 2, 9, 12, 25, 27, 39 by Martin Sanders (Beehive Illustration).

Orders: please contact Bookpoint Ltd, 130 Milton Park, Abingdon, Oxon OX14 4SB. Telephone: (44) 01235 827720. Fax: (44) 01235 400454. Lines are open from 9.00 – 6.00, Monday to Saturday, with a 24-hour message answering service. You can also order through our website www.hodderheadline.co.uk.

British Library Cataloguing in Publication Data
A catalogue record for this title is available from the British Library

ISBN 0 340 814 20 9

First Published 2004
Impression number   10 9 8 7 6 5 4 3 2 1
Year   2010 2009 2008 2007 2006 2005 2004

Cover photo shows a detail from *Dressing the Wounded During a Gas Attack* by Austin O Spare. Courtesy of The Imperial War Museum.
Typeset by Fakenham Photosetting Limited, Fakenham, Norfolk.
Printed in Dubai for Hodder & Stoughton Educational, a division of Hodder Headline, 338 Euston Road, London NW1 3BH by Oriental Press.